Magnificence of the Noble Qur'an

Prof. Dr. Taha Abideen Taha

Professor of Exegesis and Qur'an Sciences

Umm Al-Qura University, Makkah

In the name of Allah, the Most Compassionate, the Most Merciful

Introduction

All Praise be to Allah, who chose us to receive the best Scripture, sent down to the best Messenger, for the best nation that has been brought forth for mankind. He guided us with it from the ways of error, enlightened us with it out of spiritual blindness, and healed us with it from the disease of ignorance; so it was a light, guidance, healing, and mercy.

May the peace and blessings of Allah be upon our Prophet Muhammad, whose knowledge was the Qur'an, whose teaching was the Qur'an, whose call was to the Qur'an, whose character was the Qur'an, whose will and instruction was the Qur'an, and whose legacy was the Qur'an. And may the peace and blessings of Allah be upon his purified family, and his truthful Companions, and upon all those who follow their guidance until the Day of Judgment.

This is a concise treatise explaining some of the magnificence, grandeur, and exquisite beauty of the Noble Qur'an, along with its immense benefits for the people of the Qur'an. I have chosen to use easy to understand expressions, clear evidence, and various related topics. I have made it to be a rich garden, whose beautiful scent draws from the fragrance of Allah's speech in the Noble Qur'an. Its ripe fruits are easy to gather for the believers, to deepen their faith in the Book of their Lord, motivate them to recite it and ponder upon its meanings, and to act accordingly and hold firm to its teachings and guidance .The Qur'an is the best speech to be recited, the best knowledge to be learned, the most guiding light, and the best remedy for all ailments. Whoever follows it is truly guided and blissful, and whoever turns way from it is misguided and miserable. The successful one is he whom Allah guides to the companionship of the Qur'an and makes it a bliss for his heart, a delight for his eyes, and a light for his insight .I have written this treatise in a different manner than my previous books and research papers in which I would go into depth and details for the specialists in the field. As to this treatise, I aimed for a work that would be indispensable for every Muslim, whether Arab or non-Arab, young or old, male or female .The result was this treatise into which I have poured my heart out in a brief descriptive style so that every reader – by the will of Allah – finds what he is looking for in it, so that it would increase his love and reverence for the Qur'an, solidify his certitude about the truthfulness of Allah's Word, and give him more insight into it. Indeed, to open people's eyes to the magnificence of the Qur'an and its beauty, and to endear it to them and show them the way to follow its guidance and refrain from turning away from it, all this is one of the greatest deeds in life to get closer to Allah.

We ask Allah to grant us sincere truthfulness that makes our work deserving of His acceptance, and success that guides our steps, and blessing that makes this work of immense effect and benefit. Verily, He alone is able to do that, and He is the best Ally and the best Supporter.

The Word of Allah, the Glorified and Exalted

Allah Almighty says:{If any of the idolaters seek your protection, then give him refuge so that he can hear the Word of Allah}[Surat at-Tawbah : 6]The first thing that a believer should process in his belief about the Noble Qur'an is that it is the Word of Allah, so that when he directs his attention to it – whether listening to it, reciting it, or contemplating its verses – he would be mindful that he is about to experience the most sublime, most truthful, most perfect, most just, and most beautiful speech in existence. There is no truer speech in its information, nor more just speech in its rulings, nor more perfect speech in its legislations than the Qur'an. The Qur'an is the best speech memorized by the hearts of mankind, repeated by their tongues, contemplated by their intellects, and learned by the successive generations to guide them to the truth. Allah Almighty says:{Allah has sent down the best message – a consistent Book of repeated lessons –}[Surat az-Zumar: 23]Allah Almighty also says:{The Word of your Lord is perfect in truthfulness and justice; none can change His Words, and He is the All-Hearing, the All-Knowing.}[Surat al-An'ām: 115]

How can this not be true when it is the Word of the Creator of mankind, the originator and controller of all the universes throughout the ages and times? Nothing escapes Him or is hidden from Him in the heaven or on the earth. He encompasses everything with His mercy, knowledge, and wisdom. He is the Oft-Forgiving, the Loving, the Powerful, the Almighty, the Sovereign, the Great. Allah Almighty says:

{A revelation from the One Who created the earth and the high heavens.

The Most Compassionate rose over the Throne.

To Him belongs all that is in the heavens and all that is on earth, and all that is between them, and all that is beneath the soil.

Whether you speak loudly [or not], He surely knows what is secret and what is even more hidden.

Allah – none has the right to be worshiped except Him. He has the Most Beautiful Names.}

[Surat Ta Ha: 4-8]

The Qur'an is the Word of He Who has the Most Perfect Names and the Most Exalted Attributes, far above any imperfections, described with descriptions of perfection, grandeur, and beauty in all His words and actions; the High and the Magnificent. Whoever contemplates, while reading the Qur'an, that this is indeed the Word of Allah will revere every letter with utmost reverence and treat it with the utmost degree of responsibility.

Whoever approaches the Qur'an with this faith and creed rooted deeply in his heart, it will directly produce in his heart the meanings of awe, magnificence, sanctity, love, and beauty. His heart would thus be humbled, his skin would be softened [with compliance], and his body and senses would become submissive. He would be among those about whom Allah Almighty says:{causing the skins of those who fear their Lord to shiver, then their skins and their hearts soften at the remembrance of Allah.}[Surat az-Zumar: 23]Any weakness of this creed in the heart directly weakens the glorification, love, and submission to the Word of Allah. Therefore, whoever wants to have a proper relationship with the Qur'an must approach it with the belief that it is indeed the Word of Allah in truth and reality, so that reciting it and contemplating it thereafter would add to his guidance and strength of faith. The greatness of Speech arises from the greatness of the Speaker, and nothing is greater than Allah or greater than His Speech.

The Qur'an is Exalted and Protected

Allah Almighty also says: {Ha Mīm. By the Clear Book, Indeed, We have made it an Arabic Qur'an so that you may understand, and it is in the Master Book [Preserved Tablet] with us, highly esteemed, full of wisdom.}[Surat az-Zukhruf: 1-4]The Noble Qur'an is exalted in status, sublime in rank, and dignified by Allah. He placed it in the foremost and highest place of the Preserved Tablet. Allah Almighty says:{and it is in the Master Book [Preserved Tablet] with us, highly esteemed, full of wisdom.}Allah, the Glorified and Exalted, informed His slaves of that so that they would realize the status of this Book and its merit, nobleness, and immense value .Then He clarified that the Qur'an has been completely protected, cared for, and preserved in the highest assembly of angels, so that man may follow the example of that purified angels who are close to Allah in honoring the Qur'an. Rather, mankind are more worthy of honoring it and following it given that Allah revealed it to them and honored them with it. Allah Almighty says:{that this is indeed a noble Qur'an ,in a well-preserved record ,that none can touch except the purified [angels] –a revelation from the Lord of the worlds.}[Surat al-Wāqi'ah: 77-80]And He clarified the nobleness and eminence of the scrolls in which it has been written by the hands of the angels. Allah Almighty says:{[It is recorded] in honored scrolls. Exalted and purified .By the hands of scribes [angels].Noble and righteous.}[Surat 'Abasa: 13-16]Whoever contemplates these verses deeply will realize the value and status of this Book which is in our hands, and that it should be preserved with regard to the place it is kept, the paper on which it is written, the hands that carry it, and the hearts that memorize it. It is a Book of the highest status beyond what humans can imagine.Whoever understands this understands the greatness of the divine blessing and gift that Allah has bestowed on His servants by revealing this Magnificent Book. This should remind us of our negligence in its rights and our shortcomings in fulfilling our obligations towards it, and that those who turn away from it or mock it are the losers in this life and in the Hereafter.

Since the Qur'an has this special sacredness and magnificence, special rulings are legislated for its recitation and learning. We should take meticulous care to abide by them, in acknowledgment of the Qur'an's sacredness and magnificence. These rulings include purification; seeking refuge in Allah from Satan before recitation; saying 'in the name of Allah' when proceeding to recite; measured recitation; listening to its recitation attentively; and other rules. Scholars compiled many books on the etiquette that the memorizers of the Qur'an must abide by.

The Magnificence of its Descent as Revelation

Allah Almighty says:{Indeed, We sent this [Qur'an] down in the Night of Decree .How do you know what the Night of Decree is? The Night of Decree is better than a thousand months .On that night the angels and the Spirit [Gabriel] descend by their Lord's permission with all decrees .It is all peace until the break of dawn.}[Surat al-Qadr: 1-5]When Allah Almighty wanted to convey His Word to His servants, He revealed them in a manner that inspires awe and reverence. Whoever contemplates this manner of revelation understands the great value and status of this most magnificent Book. Allah revealed the Qur'an in the best month of the year [Ramadan]. Allah Almighty says:{Ramadān is a month in which the Qur'an was sent down as a guidance for mankind and as clear signs that show the right way and distinguish between right and wrong.}[Surat al-Baqarah: 185]And it was revealed in the most blessed night of that month, which is Laylat al-Qadr [the Night of Decree]. Allah Almighty says: {We sent it down in a blessed night. Indeed, We are ever warning.}[Surat ad-Dukhān: 3]And its revelation began in the best place on the face of the earth, Um al-Qura [the Mother of Villages; Makkah]. Allah Almighty says: {This is a blessed Book which We have sent down – confirming what came before it, so that you will warn the Mother of Cities [Makkah] and all those around it.}[Surat al-An'ām: 92]And He revealed it through the Greatest Angel in Heaven [Gabriel]. Allah Almighty says:{Indeed, this [Qur'an] is a word conveyed by a noble angel-messenger .extremely powerful, highly revered with the Lord of the Throne, obeyed [by other angels] and moreover, trustworthy. Your fellow [the Prophet] is not madman.}[Surat at-Takwīr: 19-22]And He revealed it to the best of the Messengers that He sent to all mankind; he was the most truthful of them in speech, the most intelligent in mind, the best in character, and the purest in heart. Allah Almighty says:{Say [O Prophet], "Whoever is an enemy to Gabriel – it is he who brings down this [Qur'an] to your heart by Allah's permission, confirming what came before it, and a guidance and glad tiding for the believers."}[Surat al-Baqarah: 97]He sent it down to the best community brought forth for mankind [the Muslim community]. Allah Almighty says:{You are the best community produced for humankind}[Surat Āl 'Imrān: 110]He revealed it in the best of languages in terms of eloquence and elucidation. Allah Almighty says:{This is indeed a revelation from the Lord of the worlds,which the Trustworthy Spirit [Gabriel] has brought down to your heart [O Prophet] so that you may be one of the warners, in clear Arabic language.}[Surat ash-Shu'arā': 192-195]These best selections of place, time, angel, messenger, community, and language indicate the greatness of the Qur'an and its superiority. They lead us to its guidance and motivate us to learn it. Rather, if someone was to consider [the similitude of] a letter sent to him by a great sovereign king of the kings of this world, or a great leader of the most eminent of leaders, by way of his trusted minister who came in person carrying the message, traveling for a year to deliver it, how would he receive the letter and the message that it contains, and how would he receive the personal messenger who brought the message to him? The Qur'an is the message from the King of all Kings, brought to us from a distance of thousands of years, carried by the most noble messenger from the angels and delivered to the most noble messenger on earth to be conveyed to us, in the most noble night of the year. Allah Almighty says:{[It is] from Allah, Master of the ways of ascent.by which the angels and the Spirit will ascend to Him on a Day the length of which is fifty thousand years.}[Surat al-Ma'ārij: 3-4]

A Heavy Word

Allah Almighty says:{We shall cast upon you a heavy word.}[Surat al-Muzzammil: 5]A heavy word means speech that is great, magnificent, precious, firmly-established, secure, and noble. All its characteristics are majestic and inspire awe and reverence. How can it be otherwise when it is the word of Allah, the Lord of the worlds?!Its heaviness is of two types: The first type: physical heaviness .This was evident at the times of its revelation to the Prophet (may Allah's peace and blessings be upon him), as he would experience a severe physical state while receiving revelation; his forehead would sweat profusely even on cold winter nights, his body would become quite heavy, and his camel would kneel to the ground when he received revelation while riding it. Once, revelation came to him while Zayd ibn Thābit (may Allah be pleased with him) was sitting next to him, and his thigh was on the thigh of Zayd who later said: "I feared that my thigh bone would crack." All of this has been transmitted through authentic narrations. It is also heavy in the Scale of deeds on the Day of Judgment and heavy in its strong impact. Allah Almighty says:{Had We sent down this Qur'an upon a mountain, you would have seen it humbled and break asunder out of awe of Allah. Such are the similitudes We set forth for people so that they may reflect.}[Surat al-Hashr: 21]The second type: moral heaviness .It is heavy on account of its weight and value, and its authenticity and eloquence. Its words are sweet, its sentences are succinct and coherent, its meanings are clear and fruitful, and its guidance is immense and beneficial. The Qur'an is inclusive of all the beliefs, obligations, penal codes, and rulings that man needs. Moreover, it is completely free of idle talk, improper language, crookedness, and worthless matters. Allah Almighty says:{It is an Arabic Qur'an, free of flaws and contradictions, so that they may be conscious of Allah.}[Surat az-Zumar: 28]It is also heavy for the minds to fully grasp its meanings, benefits, and guidance. It is heavy to fully act upon it in terms of the penal codes and obligations it ordains, except for those whom Allah Almighty made it easy, for them it is easy. It is heavy on the disbelievers and the hypocrites, because it exposes their secrets, lies, deception and corruptions. It weakens them and gives them stern warnings that strike terror into their hearts. Allah Almighty says:{Even if there were a Qur'an that could cause mountains to move, or split the earth, or cause the dead to speak, [they would still not believe]. To Allah belongs all matters. Do the believers not know that if Allah had willed, He could have guided all humans?...}[Surat ar-Ra'd: 31]Whoever does not feel the heaviness of Allah's Speech – while reciting, contemplating, and following it – must review soundness of his faith, for it is this feeling of heaviness that makes the believers earn the status described by Allah, as in the following verse:{This is a Qur'an that We have revealed over stages so that you may recite it to people at a slower pace, and We have sent it down in a successive manner .Say, "Believe in it, or do not believe. Those who were given knowledge before it, when it is recited to them, they fall on their faces in prostration and they say, "Glory be to our Lord. The promise of our Lord is bound to be fulfilled." They fall down on their faces weeping, and it increases their humility."}[Surat al-Isrā': 106-109]And whoever realizes its heaviness realizes the enormity of the responsibility he is entrusted with. Allah Almighty says: {Indeed, We offered the Trust to the heavens, the earth, and the mountains, yet they refused to bear it and were afraid of it. But man assumed it; he is indeed wrongful and ignorant.}[Surat al-Ahzāb: 72]So hasten to avoid the wrongdoing of distancing yourself from the Qur'an and being ignorant of its contents, so that you would be able to carry its weight.

There is no Doubt Therein

Allah Almighty says:{This is the Book about which there is no doubt, a guidance for the righteous.}[Surat al-Baqarah: 2]One of the fundamentals of faith that must be firmly planted in the hearts the way mountains are firmly planted in the earth is to believe that the Noble Qur'an is the truth without any doubt, a revelation from Allah, Lord of the worlds. It is not the words of a poet or a soothsayer or a magician, or something fabricated by Muhammad (may Allah's peace and blessings be upon him), or something that he copied from past scriptures. Allah Almighty says: {[This is] the revelation of the Book about which there is no doubt from the Lord of the worlds.}[Surat as-Sajdah: 1]Negating doubt about it in this context is general. The word 'doubt' is not preceded by a definite article, so (according to Arabic grammar rules) it indicates that the negation is general, extending to all the contents of the Qur'an, whether information, rulings, or guidance, and to every verse and letter therein. Allah Almighty says:{So be not in doubt about it. It is the Truth from your Lord, but most people do not believe.}[Surat Hud:

17]The general negation of doubt also extends to all its logical arguments and proofs that indicate its truthfulness and certainty. The general negation entails attestation to the permanence of the authenticity of its source, the perfection of its guidance, the soundness of its arguments, and its infallibility against errors and flaws. There is no place for any doubt about it in any aspect in all times and places. It is thus distinguished from other divine Scriptures which are not free from doubt due to the distortions that occurred to them. Those who doubt its source or any of its contents, they are either a people who are ignorant of its truth and who deny what they do not understand, as Allah says about them:{But they rejected that which they did not comprehend, and its warning has not yet been fulfilled against them. Similarly, those who came before them refused to believe. Then see how was the end of the wrongdoers!}[Surat Yūnus: 39]Or, they are people who do know its truth, but they deny it out of stubbornness and arrogance, or they follow their personal desires, so they sell their religion in return for a petty worldly gain. Allah Almighty says: {And do not trade my verses for a small price. And fear only Me.}[Surat al-Baqarah: 41]Allah, the Truthful, addresses them with what eliminates doubtful allegations from their hearts, by clarifying the miraculous nature of the Qur'an which conclusively negates attributing it to other than Allah. Allah Almighty says:{If you are in doubt concerning that which We have sent down upon Our slave, then produce a chapter like it and call upon your helpers other than Allah, if you are truthful . But if you did not do it, and you can never do it; then beware of the Fire whose fuel will be people and stones, which is prepared for the disbelievers.}[Surat al-Baqarah: 23-24]By these verses, Allah proves the impotency of the Arabs to produce the like of its shortest chapter, which is decisive proof that non-Arabs would not be able to do that with greater reason [given that the Arabs are eloquent native speakers of Arabic, the language of the Qur'an]. Negating doubt about the Qur'an entails complete trust in its source and confidence that all its contents are true and just. It also entails resorting to it to settle disputes, absolute submission to it, and full acceptance of its guidance.

A Verification and a Criterion

Allah Almighty says:{And We have revealed to you the Book in truth, confirming that which preceded it of the Scripture and as a criterion over it.}[Surat al-Mā'idah: 48]When Allah wanted to finalize the sending of messengers and messages, He concluded them with this precious Book which confirms the scriptures that came before it and has final authority over them, and it abrogates all religions other than Islam. So it confirmed the veracity of the scriptures that were revealed to the prophets of Allah, like the Torah, Psalms and Gospel and other scriptures, as it called to everything that those scriptures called for of the fundamentals of belief, morals, and modes of worship. Allah Almighty says:{This Qur'an could not possibly have been produced by anyone other than Allah. It is a confirmation of what came before it and an explanation of the Scripture, and is undoubtedly from the Lord of the worlds.}[Surat Yūnus: 37]The Qur'an has authority over those scriptures as it corrects and sets aright what occurred in them of distortion. Whatever the Qur'an confirms of the contents of past scriptures is true and correct, and whatever the Qur'an denies is false and invalid, even if the followers of those scriptures believe otherwise. Allah Almighty says:{The Jews say, "Ezra is the son of Allah," and the Christians say, "The Messiah is the son of Allah." These are mere words that they utter, imitating the words of the disbelievers before them. May Allah ruin them; how can they be deluded? They have taken their rabbis and monks as lords besides Allah, as well as the Messiah, son of Mary, even though they were commanded to worship only One God; none has the right to be worshiped except Him, glorified is He far above what they associate with Him.}[Surat at-Tawbah: 30-31]Thus Allah exposed the lies and distortions in their scriptures concerning false beliefs, false forms and objects of worship, and other matters. Such confirmation of past scriptures and authority over them are a clear indication of the greatness of the Qur'an and its magnificent status, and that it is the best of all revealed scriptures, containing the essence and summary of all that preceded it and more. Allah Almighty says:{And indeed, it is [mentioned] in the scriptures of former peoples.}[Surat ash-Shu'arā': 196]And therefore, the Qur'an is the best of speech:{Allah has sent down the best message...}[Surat az-Zumar: 23] If this fact is established in the heart of the worshiper of Allah, he will run to the Qur'an and not run away from it to any other book, because he knows that it is his salvation. This is why Allah says to us:{And follow the best of what was revealed to you from your Lord... }[Surat az-Zumar: 55]And, without doubt, the best of what was revealed is the noble Qur'an. This great honor that Allah assigned exclusively to the Qur'an should make it dearer to us and should make us adhere more firmly to its guidance and believe with certitude that it is the source of our distinction and the secret behind the strength and continual vitality of this nation. This greatly increases the believer's love for the Qur'an and its glorification. He would not be dazzled by the decadent aspects of Western civilization or by what the enemies of the Muslim nation propagate of lies and malicious allegations about some of the teachings of the Qur'an as a result of their failure to understand their wisdom and greatness.

Eternal Preservation

Allah Almighty says:{And it is indeed a Mighty Book. No falsehood can approach it from the front or from behind; a revelation from the One Who is All-Wise, Praiseworthy.}[Surat Fussilat: 41-42]Since the Noble Qur'an is the final message from Allah, and the Messenger who conveyed it is the final Messenger, Allah Almighty himself undertook the responsibility to preserve it, so He guarded it from any alteration, corruption, or distortion. Allah Almighty says:{It is We Who have sent down the Reminder, and it is We Who will preserve it.}[Surat al-Hijr: 9]Allah Almighty preserved it against perishing and against any attempts of addition, reduction, distortion, or alteration. This is a distinctive characteristic that Allah assigned to the Qur'an apart from all the other scriptures that He entrusted to some of His creation, but they were altered and distorted. Allah Almighty says:{... and those that were entrusted to preserve the scripture and were witnesses to it...}[Surat al-Mā'idah: 44]You will not find in existence a book that has been preserved in its honor and its exact words, and has been protected from any doubt of alterations, like this Book. Allah Almighty says:{Recite what has been revealed to you from the Book of your Lord. None can change His Words, and you will never find any refuge except with Him.}[Surat al-Kahf: 27] So, do not listen to the allegations of the doomed Shi'a Rejectionists and those who followed them in their clear misguidance, those who seek to belie what Allah has stated unequivocally. They are in opposition to what the Muslims have unanimously agreed upon from the earliest generations to the present time. How could what Allah Almighty Himself preserved be altered? Allah threatened whoever considers to do that to cut his aorta (which is the lifeline for any human being). Allah Almighty says:{It is a revelation from the Lord of the worlds .If he had falsely attributed something to Us, We would have surely seized him by the right hand , then severed his aorta, and none of you could have rescued him.}[Surat al-Huqqah: 43-47]This preservation of the Qur'an existed in all its stages; when it was revealed, powerful guards and burning flames were made to guard the heavens from the jinn who sought to listen and eavesdrop thereof, as Allah Almighty says:{We have sought to reach the heaven but found it filled with stern guards and flaming fire . We used to take up positions there for eavesdropping, but now anyone who eavesdrops will find a flaming fire waiting for him.}[Surat al-Jinn: 8-9]And Allah also preserved it in the heart of the Prophet (may Allah's peace and blessings be upon him) during its revelation to him, as Allah Almighty says:{Do not move your tongue [O Prophet] in haste trying to memorize it. It is upon Us to make you memorize and recite it.}[Surat al-Qiyāmah: 16-17]Then Allah Almighty undertook to preserve it Himself after the completion of its revelation so that it remains eternal until Allah raises it to Heaven at the end of time. The Qur'an has remained in its preserved pristine state throughout these long centuries despite the catastrophes that the Muslim nation has gone through. This reveals another aspect of the magnificence of this noble Book, whose eternalness keeps the message of Islam eternal.

The Most Miraculous Sign of the Message of Islam

Allah Almighty says:{If you are in doubt concerning that which We have sent down upon Our slave, then produce a chapter like it and call upon your helpers other than Allah, if you are truthful. But if you did not do it, and you can never do it; then beware of the Fire whose fuel will be people and stones, which is prepared for the disbelievers.}[Surat al-Baqarah: 24-25]Allah did not send any messenger except that He sent with him a miracle to prove his truthfulness and to support his mission. All of these messengers had tangible miracles, except Prophet Muhammad (may Allah's peace and blessings be upon him).Allah made his miracle intangible and abstract through this Noble Book that He revealed to him. It is from one aspect a book of guidance and from another a miracle proving the truthfulness of Muhammad's message. Allah Almighty says:{...a guidance for mankind and as clear signs that show the right way and distinguish between right and wrong.}[Surat al-Baqarah: 185]On account of the revelation of the Qur'an, the Prophet (may Allah's peace and blessings be upon him) hoped that his nation of believers following him would be the largest nation on the Day of Judgment. Al-Bukhāri and Muslim narrated that he says: "There was no prophet among the prophets but was given miracles because of which people had faith and believed in them, but what I was given is the Divine Inspiration which Allah revealed to me. So I hope that my followers will be more than those of any other prophet on the Day of Resurrection. "Allah challenged all of the antagonists and opponents, to bring a similar revelation, but they were all incapable and impotent, as Allah Almighty says:{Say, "If all humans and jinn were to come together to produce something similar to this Qur'an, they would not be able to produce the like of it, even if they collaborated with one another."}[Surat al-Isrā': 88]Then Allah challenged them to produce only ten chapters of its like, as Allah Almighty says:{Or do they say, "He has fabricated it"? Say, "Then produce ten fabricated Chapters like it and seek help from whoever you can besides Allah, if you are truthful!"}[Surat Hud: 13]Then Allah challenged them to produce just one chapter like it, and they were unable. Allah Almighty says: {Or do they say, "He fabricated it?" Say, "Produce then one Chapter like it, and call upon whoever you can other than Allah, if you are truthful!"}[Surat Yūnus: 38] He then challenged them to bring even one similar chapter and told them decisively that they were not able to do that and would never be able to do it, so they were utterly defeated in their incapacity. This was unequivocal evidence of the truthfulness of the message throughout the ages and ample proof for whoever desires to find guidance. Allah Almighty says:{Is it not enough for them that We have sent down to you the Book which is being recited to them? Indeed, there is a mercy and reminder in it for people who believe.}[Surat al-'Ankabūt: 51]Therefore, whoever is not guided by the Qur'an with its miraculous aspects being sufficient for him as a sign and proof, then nothing else can guide him. Allah Almighty says:{In which message after this [Qur'an] will they believe?}[Surat al-Mursalāt: 50]

The renowned Arab poet Ahmad Shawqi said in his famous poem about the Prophet (may Allah's peace and blessings be upon him):

The prophets came with miracles, and they all have elapsed,

And you came to us with a wise scripture that never elapses,

Its verses, as time passes, are ever new,

Adorned by the magnificence of ancientness.

A Clarification for all Things

Allah Almighty says:{We have sent down to you the Book as an explanation of everything, and as a guidance, mercy and glad tidings for the Muslims.}[Surat an-Nahl: 89]The noble Qur'an is the only Book of scripture that satisfies all the needs of mankind in all aspects of life in a way that reforms all the affairs of their religion, worldly life, and afterlife; in their personal, social, and civilizational spheres; in the aspects of creed, worship, morality, politics, economy, society, etc. This is the mercy and blessing of Allah upon them. The distinctive characteristic of fulfilling the various needs of man is not found in any scripture other than the Qur'an. Allah Almighty says:{And We have sent down to you the Book as clarification for all things}Allah Almighty also says:{We have missed nothing in the Book}[Surat al-An'ām: 38]This understanding is based on the interpretation that the Book mentioned in the verses is the Qur'an, and the context indicates to this meaning.

Since the guidance of the Qur'an as an explanation of all things includes two categories of verses: one is clear-cut and easily understood and another is implicit and needs a degree of analysis and discerning to comprehend it. Muslim scholars have worked diligently throughout history to extract its diverse sciences which are too many to count, to the extent that no book in the history of mankind has ever had as many books and works written about it as the Noble Qur'an. It is the most prolific of all the revealed scriptures in terms of its content of knowledge, guidance, and wise instructions, and in commanding every form of goodness and forbidding every form of evil. All of its commands and rulings are established upon justice, mercy, and wisdom, completely sufficing mankind's needs and necessities.

This is another avenue to appreciate the magnificence of the Qur'an, since no other book comprehensively encompasses all the knowledge that mankind needs for guidance. This makes us, as we recite its verses and explore its wisdom, realize that we are before an ocean of knowledge that has no shore, and that this immense guidance never ceases to give new insights and perspectives. It is for this reason that the scholars in every era rush to the Qur'an to seek guidance from it whenever they are faced with a difficulty or a controversy. They reflect upon its verses to find guidance therein. Not a single one of those scholars ever claimed that his knowledge and comprehension encompassed all of the Qur'an; rather, all of them admit their limitations in this regard. Whenever the applied and intellectual sciences of life achieve new frontiers, we find that none of the new advancements conflict with the Qur'an; rather, the Qur'an verifies it, confirming over and over again that the Qur'an is proof of its own truthfulness and that it is from the One Whose Knowledge encompasses everything. Allah Almighty says:{We will show them Our signs in the universe and in their own selves, until it becomes clear to them that this [Qur'an] is the truth. Is it not enough that your Lord is a Witness over all things?}[Surat Fussilat: 53]

The Magnificence of the Names and Attributes of the Qur'an

Allah Almighty says:{O mankind, there has come to you an exhortation from your Lord, a cure for [illness] of the hearts, a guidance and mercy for the believers.}[Yūnus: 57]The variety of names and attributes given to the Qur'an indicates the magnificence and beauty of this glorious Book. There are so many names and attributes for the Qur'an that some scholars have written complete books on this subject. One of these names is 'al-Kitāb' (the Book). Allah Almighty says:{This is the Book about which there is no doubt, a guidance for the righteous.}[Surat al-Baqarah: 2]If the 'Book' is mentioned, the meaning is the Qur'an, for there is no other book that comes even close to the traits of this Book, let alone be equal to it. Another name is 'al-Furqān' (the Criterion) because the Qur'an is the criterion which separates truth from falsehood. Allah Almighty says:{Blessed is He Who sent down the Criterion upon His Servant so that it may be a warning to all people.}[Surat al-Furqān: 1]Another name is 'al-Haqq' (the Truth), as Allah Almighty says:{As for those who believe, do righteous deeds, and believe in what has been sent down to Muhammad – which is the truth from their Lord – He will absolve them of their sins and set their condition right.}[Surat Muhammad: 2]Another name is 'al-'Ilm' (the Knowledge) because it contains all the knowledge of the previous scriptures and then more, as Allah Almighty says:{If you were to follow their desires after the knowledge that has come to you, then you would have no protector or helper against Allah.}[Surat al-Baqarah: 120]Another name is 'al-Huda' (the Guidance), as the jinn called it when they heard it being recited. Allah Almighty says:{And when we heard the guidance we believed in it... }[Surat al-Jinn: 13]And another name is 'an-Noor' (the Light). Allah Almighty says: {So believe in Allah and His Messenger, and in the Light [the Qur'an] that We have sent down.}[Surat at-Taghābun: 8]And from the names of the Qur'an is 'al-Dhikr' (the Remembrance/the Reminder). Allah Almighty says:{Indeed, it is We Who sent down the Reminder, and it is We Who will preserve it.}[Surat al-Hijr: 9]And the Qur'an has many other names. And just as the various names indicate the magnificence and beauty of the Qur'an, so do its many traits and descriptions. Among the adjectives that Allah used to describe the Qur'an is that it is 'Karim' (noble, generous). Allah Almighty says:{Indeed, it is a noble Qur'an.}[Surat al-Wāqi'ah: 77]Another trait is "Azhīm' (great, magnificent). Allah Almighty says:{We have surely given you the seven oft-repeated verses and the great Qur'an.}[Surat al-Hijr: 87]Another description is 'Hakīm' (wise). Allah Almighty says: {By the wise Qur'an.}[Surat Ya Sīn: 2]And He described it as 'Majīd' (glorious, praised). Allah Almighty says: {Qāf. By the glorious Qur'an.}[Surat Qāf: 1]And another trait is "Azīz' (mighty, honored in rank, powerful). Allah Almighty says:{...and most surely it is a mighty Book.}[Surat Fussilat: 41]The Qur'an has many other attributes. If you contemplate them, you will realize that each one of them individually suffices to indicate the greatness of the Qur'an and the gloriousness of its merits, and encourages the seeker to study it and teach it to others. When there are many beautiful names and sublime attributes for an entity, this indicates its greatness. How great would it then be if it has more than a hundred of the best descriptions, including that it is light, spirit, truth, guidance, healing, mercy, noble, wise, great, magnificent, and others.

A Book of Wisdom

Allah Almighty says:{This is what We recite to you of the verses and wise reminder.}[Surat Āl 'Imrān: 58]The Qur'an is the wise Book whose verses abound in wisdom. How could it be otherwise when it is the revelation from the All-Wise, the All-Knowledgeable, the All-Aware Lord, Sovereign of the Universe. Allah Almighty says:{Alif Lām Ra. This is a Book whose verses are perfected, then fully explained, from One Who is All-Wise, All-Aware.}[Surat Hud: 1]Allah Almighty also says:{Indeed, you are receiving the Qur'an from the All-Wise, All-Knowing.}[Surat an-Naml: 6]It is therefore a Book of decisive wise words, with wisdom in all its aspects in terms of content, method of instruction, order of priorities, diverse styles, and many other aspects. Since the Qur'an encompasses all aspects of wisdom, describing it as 'Wise' has become inseparable from it. In fact, Allah Almighty describes it as 'Wise' in several verses. Allah says:{Alif, Lām, Ra. These are the verses of the wise Book.}[Surat Yūnus: 1]Allah Almighty also says:{Alif, Lām, Mīm.These are the verses of the wise Book. A guidance and mercy for those who do good.}[Surat Luqmān: 1-3]Allah also says:{Ya Sīn.And the wise Book.}[Surat Ya Sīn: 1-2]From among the various facets of the perfect wisdom of the Qur'an is the fact that desires are not deviated by it but are rather guided; tongues are not confused by it, opinions are not scattered about it, scholars never get fully satisfied seeking out its meanings; righteous people never become weary of it; and its amazing features never cease to fascinate. Whoever learns its knowledge surpasses others, whoever speaks according to it is truthful, whoever judges according to it is just, whoever acts according to it is rewarded, and whoever calls to it is guided to a straight path. Any person who takes the Qur'an as his guide attains thereby the most perfect human characteristics and eternal happiness, because it is by the Qur'an that one attains truth in beliefs, words and actions; and it rectifies behavior and uplifts souls. It is the book that produces wise people and grants wisdom. For this reason, Ibn 'Abbās (may Allah be pleased with him and his father) said about the saying of Allah, the Exalted:{He grants wisdom to whom He wills... }[Surat al-Baqarah: 269]"Wisdom is understanding the Noble Qur'an."[Narrated by At-Tabari in his Tafsīr (exegesis)]It is the source of wisdom and guidance that rectifies words and deeds, and prohibits corruption and evil. Whoever makes the Qur'an his starting point, wisdom will shield him, and he will truly be a sage. Whoever realizes the perfection of the pearls of wisdom in the Qur'an would not seek to study other books written by western philosophers and thinkers or others who are called people of wisdom. He will come to know the shallowness of their opinions because he will realize that there is no aspect of goodness except that Allah Almighty clarified it in the Qur'an, called people to it, and encouraged them to seek it. He mentioned the aspects of wisdom and benefit that invite people to it. And there is not any aspect of evil or corruption but He explained it, warned against it, and prohibited it, and He mentioned the reasons why it should be avoided and its harmful consequences. So, whoever is guided to the Qur'an is indeed guided to the path of wisdom whose followers are promised abundant good by Allah Almighty in His saying: {...and whoever is given wisdom is surely given abundant good, but none will take heed except people of understanding.}[Surat al-Baqarah: 269]

A Blessed Remembrance

Allah Almighty says:{And this [Qur'an] is a blessed reminder which We have sent down. Will you then deny it?}[Surat al-Anbiyā': 50]The value of any book is proved by the benefits it entails and the influence it has on people. One of the greatest attributes with which Allah described His Book is that it is a 'Blessed Book', meaning: it is full of blessings; it has perpetual good within it; its benefit is continuous in the life of this world, the life of the grave, and in the Hereafter. Its information and sciences are diverse; its guidance is infinite; the reward for learning it and teaching it is abundant; whoever adheres to its guidance will be blessed in this life and in the afterlife. For all of these reasons, Allah describes for the believers what they will gain by adhering to its teachings. Allah Almighty says:{And this Book We have revealed it, a blessing, so follow it and fear Allah so that you may be shown mercy.}[Surat al-An'ām: 155]From among its many blessings is that it appeals to the hearts and heals them, and purifies the souls. It guides to the truth and destroys falsehood, drives away the devils, brings about justice and mercy, and exalts the reminder. No one can deny these blessings except an arrogant obstinate person. Allah Almighty says:{And this [Qur'an] is a blessed reminder which We have revealed. Will you then deny it?}[Surat al-Anbiyā': 50]And from among its many blessings is that all the benefits of the past Scriptures are contained within it and more. Allah Almighty says:{And this is a blessed Book that We have sent down, confirming that which came before it... }[Surat al-An'ām: 92]Whoever knows the blessings of this Book in its divine origin and its exalted meanings and sciences, will realize the immense benefits and blessings it brings to those who recite it or in their homes or those who listen to it, contemplate its meanings, learn it and teach it, and serve it. Allah Almighty says:{This is a blessed Book which We have revealed to you so that they may contemplate its verses, and so that people of reason may be mindful.}[Surat Sād: 29]It is a blessed Book, full of benefits for those who accompany it in their lives, and those who follow it, act according to its teachings and give their life to serve it. No one sincerely and faithfully reads it and acts by it except that he will have a good life, a good and noble character, a life of magnanimity, and a soul full of delight and satisfaction. These blessings surround this person from all walks of his life, and every day he increases in blessings and improves in development. Whoever experiences this reality, knows its truth, and how can it be otherwise, when he is in the company of this blessed divine companion, the Book of Allah. Just reading one chapter will bring him blessings, as narrated in Sahih Muslim that the Prophet (may Allah's peace and blessings be upon him) said :"Recite Surat al-Baqarah, for taking recourse to it is a blessing, and abandoning it is a cause of grief, and the sorcerers cannot confront it."

A Reminder to the Worlds

Allah Almighty says:{It is not but a reminder to the worlds.}[Surat Sād: 87]One of the most magnificent characteristics of this glorious Book is the inclusiveness of its message, addressing mankind and jinn, regardless of their race, color, or language, and regardless of their geographic location or the era they live in. It is not as what some opponents of Islam try to propagate - that it is only for Arabs. Yes, it was revealed in clear Arabic language, but its guidance is for all mankind until the Day of Judgment. Allah Almighty says:{Blessed is He who sent down the Criterion upon His Servant, so that it may be a warning to all people.}[Surat al-Furqān: 1]Hence, its message addresses all of mankind. Allah Almighty says:{O mankind, worship your Lord, Who created you and those who came before you, so that you may fear Allah.}[Surat al-Baqarah:21]Allah Almighty also says:{... a guidance for mankind and clear proofs of guidance and criterion between right and wrong.}[Surat al-Baqarah: 185]It is a book that recounts the history of mankind from the creation of the first human, Adam (peace be upon him) and his descent to earth, until the last and final messenger, the Prophet Muhammad (may Allah's peace and blessings be upon him). It explains to mankind their common origin and destroys the prejudices of nationalism and tribalism and others to establish its life on a firm basis of unity and guide it to a straight path. Allah Almighty says:{O mankind, We have created you from a male and a female, and made you into nations and tribes so that you may recognize one another. Indeed, the most noble of you before Allah is the most righteous among you. Indeed, Allah is All-Knowing, All-Aware.}[Surat al-Hujurāt: 13]It is One Book with which Allah Almighty addresses both jinn and mankind in all times and all places, for Allah is the Lord of the worlds, and the Qur'an is the revealed Book of the Lord of the worlds, Who alone knows what is beneficial for all creation. His guidance is not limited to any particular time or place, or any particular race or color of people. He guides to the Truth in creed and belief, to the finest moral principles and character, and to the best laws and legal codes that set their life aright. Allah Almighty says:{This Qur'an could not possibly have been produced by anyone other than Allah. It is a confirmation of what came before it and an explanation of the Scripture, and is undoubtedly from the Lord of the worlds.}[Surat Yūnus: 37]Allah Almighty also says:{[This is] the revelation of the Book about which there is no doubt from the Lord of the worlds.}[Surat as-Sajdah: 2]Allah Almighty also says:{They are those whom Allah has guided, so follow their guidance. Say, "I do not ask any reward for it. It is but a reminder for the worlds."}[Surat al-An'ām: 90]Whoever understands this meaning realizes the magnificence of this Book and the religion of Islam and works to serve the message that Allah sent for everyone to grant them His mercy, light, and guidance.

[Surat al-An'ām: 90]

Whoever understands this meaning realizes the magnificence of this Book and the religion of Islam and works to serve the message that Allah sent for everyone to grant them His mercy, light, and guidance.

A Spirit by the Command of Allah

Allah Almighty says: {Likewise We have revealed to you a revelation by Our command. You knew nothing of the Scripture or matters of faith, but We have made it [the Qur'an] a light by which We guide whom We will of Our slaves. And you are truly leading people to a straight path.}[Surat ash-Shūra: 52]Allah Almighty brought us to life with two spirits: one is the spirit for the physical aspects, which is the soul that gives life to the bodies. Allah Almighty says: {They ask you [O Prophet] about the soul. Say, "The soul is only known to my Lord.}[Surat al-Isrā': 85]The other is a moral spirit that gives spiritual life to the hearts. Allah Almighty says: {He sent down the angels with the Spirit by His command, unto whom He wills of His servants} [Surat an-Nahl: 2] The intended meaning here is that Allah sends down the angels with the revelation upon those whom He wills of His slaves, and He makes them prophets and messengers. Allah Almighty says:{And thus We have inspired to you a Spirit by Our command}The Qur'an is the only book of scripture which truly brings life to the hearts and inspires the spirit of faith in the universe. Therefore, Allah Almighty says:{O You who believe, respond to Allah and the Messenger when he calls you to what gives you life.}[Surat al-Anfāl: 24]Allah Almighty also says:{Is the one who was dead and We gave him life [by faith] and gave him a light with which he walks among people like the one in darkness from which he can never escape?}[Surat al-An'ām: 122]Just like the earth that comes to life after rain from the sky, as Allah Almighty says:{... You see the land lifeless, then as soon as We send down rain on it, it stirs and swells to life and brings forth every type of pleasant plant..}[Surat al-Hajj: 5]Likewise, you will find some nations lost in their misguidance, lifeless, and distressed when they are without the Qur'an, and then, when the light of the Qur'an shines on them, they are awakened and they spring forth to grow into every delightful kind of successful development. This is the case of the Arabs who were utterly lost before Islam, and then after the Qur'an came to them they produced the best role models for mankind. From all of the above, it becomes clear to us the merit of this Book and its value and influence in the lives of individuals and societies. The most perfect people are those who most perfectly follow it and respond to it. The best societies, with the highest status, are those that best live by it. For this reason, the Prophet (may Allah's peace and blessings be upon him) said: "Indeed, Allah elevates some people with this Book and degrades thereby others." [Narrated by Muslim]. Therefore, whoever embraces the Qur'an, it will raise his status and honor, and it will give him a good pleasant life. And whoever turns away from it, or believes in some parts and disbelieves in other parts, Allah will degrade him, make him miserable, and seize him. Allah Almighty says:{Do you then believe in part of the Scripture and deny another part? Then what is the recompense for those who do so among you except disgrace in this life, and on the Day of Resurrection they will be subjected to the severest torment? For Allah is not unaware of what you do.}[Surat al-Baqarah: 85]Allah Almighty also says:{But whoever turns away from My Reminder will have a miserable life, and on the Day of Resurrection We will raise him blind."}[Surat Ta Ha: 124]

{Likewise We have revealed to you a revelation by Our command. You knew nothing of the Scripture or matters of faith, but We have made it [the Qur'an] a light by which We guide whom We will of Our slaves. And you are truly leading people to a straight path.}

[Surat ash-Shūra: 52]

Allah Almighty brought us to life with two spirits: one is the spirit for the physical aspects, which is the soul that gives life to the bodies. Allah Almighty says:

{They ask you [O Prophet] about the soul. Say, "The soul is only known to my Lord.}

[Surat al-Isrā': 85]

The other is a moral spirit that gives spiritual life to the hearts. Allah Almighty says:

{He sent down the angels with the Spirit by His command, unto whom He wills of His servants}

[Surat an-Nahl: 2]

The intended meaning here is that Allah sends down the angels with the revelation upon those whom He wills of His slaves, and He makes them prophets and messengers. Allah Almighty says:

{And thus We have inspired to you a Spirit by Our command}

The Qur'an is the only book of scripture which truly brings life to the hearts and inspires the spirit of faith in the universe. Therefore, Allah Almighty says:

{O You who believe, respond to Allah and the Messenger when he calls you to what gives you life.}

[Surat al-Anfāl: 24]

Allah Almighty also says:

{Is the one who was dead and We gave him life [by faith] and gave him a light with which he walks among people like the one in darkness from which he can never escape?}

[Surat al-An'ām: 122]

Just like the earth that comes to life after rain from the sky, as Allah Almighty says:

{... You see the land lifeless, then as soon as We send down rain on it, it stirs and swells to life and brings forth every type of pleasant plant..}

[Surat al-Hajj: 5]

Likewise, you will find some nations lost in their misguidance, lifeless, and distressed when they are without the Qur'an, and then, when the light of the Qur'an shines on them, they are awakened and they spring forth to grow into every delightful kind of successful development. This is the case of the Arabs who were utterly lost before Islam, and then after the Qur'an came to them they produced the best role models for mankind.

From all of the above, it becomes clear to us the merit of this Book and its value and influence in the lives of individuals and societies. The most perfect people are those who most perfectly follow it and respond to it. The best societies, with the highest status, are those that best live by it. For this reason, the Prophet (may Allah's peace and blessings be upon him) said:

"Indeed, Allah elevates some people with this Book and degrades thereby others." [Narrated by Muslim]

Therefore, whoever embraces the Qur'an, it will raise his status and honor, and it will give him a good pleasant life. And whoever turns away from it, or believes in some parts and disbelieves in other parts, Allah will degrade him, make him miserable, and seize him. Allah Almighty says:

{Do you then believe in part of the Scripture and deny another part? Then what is the recompense for those who do so among you except disgrace in this life, and on the Day of Resurrection they will be subjected to the severest torment? For Allah is not unaware of what you do.}

[Surat al-Baqarah: 85]

Allah Almighty also says:

{But whoever turns away from My Reminder will have a miserable life, and on the Day of Resurrection We will raise him blind."}

[Surat Ta Ha: 124]

But We Made it a Light

Allah Almighty says: {Likewise We have revealed to you a revelation by Our command. You knew nothing of the Scripture or matters of faith, but We have made it [the Qur'an] a light by which We guide whom We will of Our slaves.}[Surat ash-Shūra: 52]Allah Almighty illuminated our existence with two lights for our guidance; a physical light and a spiritual light. The physical light is through the sun and the moon. Allah Almighty says: {and He placed the moon as a light in them [the skies] and the sun as a burning lamp}[Surat Nūh: 16]And the spiritual light is through the Qur'an and Sunnah. Allah Almighty says: {So believe in Allah and His Messenger, and in the Light [the Qur'an] that We have sent down. And Allah is All-Aware of what you do.}[Surat at-Taghābun: 8]Allah Almighty also says:{O mankind, there has come to you a conclusive proof from your Lord, and We have sent down to you a clear light.}[Surat an-Nisā': 174]The physical light guides the physical faculty of sight, and the spiritual light guides the spiritual insight of the souls, which is more important, since by this a person can discern the truth. Allah Almighty says:{There has surely come to you from Allah a light and a clear Book through which Allah guides those who seek His pleasure to the ways of peace, and brings them out of the depths of darkness to the light by His Will, and guides them to a straight path.}[Surat al-Mā'idah: 15-16]Allah Almighty also says:{Alif Lām Ra. This is a book that We have sent down to you, so that you may bring people out of the depths of darkness into the light, by their Lord's permission, to the path of the All-Mighty, the Praiseworthy.}[Surat Ibrāhīm:1]Allah also says:{He is the One Who sends down clear verses to His slave to bring you out of the depths of darkness into the light. Indeed, Allah is Ever Gracious and Most Merciful to you.}[Surat al-Hadīd: 9]This is the light by which Allah brings His allies from the darkness of misguidance to the light of guidance. Allah Almighty says:{Allah is the ally of those who believe; He brings them out from darkness into the light.}[Surat al-Baqarah: 257]Allah Almighty also says:{He is the One Who sends down clear verses to His slave to bring you out of the depths of darkness into the light. Indeed, Allah is Ever Gracious and Most Merciful to you.}[Surat al-Hadīd: 9]And it is the light that leads to success in this life and the Hereafter. Allah Almighty says:{So those who believe in him, they honor and support him, and follow the light which is sent down with him – it is they who will be successful."}[Surat al-A'rāf: 157]And it is the light by which a believer walks among people with insight and discernment in life. Allah Almighty says:{Is the one who was dead and We gave him life [by faith] and gave him a light with which he walks among people like the one in darkness from which he can never escape?}[Surat al-An'ām: 122]The guidance of the Qur'an is the light by which the believer crosses the Sirāt (the Bridge over Hellfire that all must pass over) on the Day of Resurrection. Allah Almighty says:{On the Day when you will see the believing men and the believing women, with their light streaming out ahead of them and to their right…}[Surat al-Hadīd: 12]

{Likewise, we have revealed to you a revelation by Our command. You knew nothing of the Scripture or matters of faith, but We have made it [the Qur'an] a light by which We guide whom We will of Our slaves.}

[Surat ash-Shūra: 52]

Allah Almighty illuminated our existence with two lights for our guidance; a physical light and a spiritual light. The physical light is through the sun and the moon. Allah Almighty says:

{and He placed the moon as a light in them [the skies] and the sun as a burning lamp}

[Surat Nūh: 16]

And the spiritual light is through the Qur'an and Sunnah. Allah Almighty says:

{So believe in Allah and His Messenger, and in the Light [the Qur'an] that We have sent down. And Allah is All-Aware of what you do.}

[Surat at-Taghābun: 8]

Allah Almighty also says:

{O mankind, there has come to you a conclusive proof from your Lord, and We have sent down to you a clear light.}

[Surat an-Nisā': 174]

The physical light guides the physical faculty of sight, and the spiritual light guides the spiritual insight of the souls, which is more important, since by this a person can discern the truth. Allah Almighty says:

{There has surely come to you from Allah a light and a clear Book

through which Allah guides those who seek His pleasure to the ways of peace, and brings them out of the depths of darkness to the light by His Will, and guides them to a straight path.}

[Surat al-Mā'idah: 15-16]

Allah Almighty also says:

{Alif Lām Ra. This is a book that We have sent down to you, so that you may bring people out of the depths of darkness into the light, by their Lord's permission, to the path of the All-Mighty, the Praiseworthy.}

[Surat Ibrāhīm:1]

Allah also says:

{He is the One Who sends down clear verses to His slave to bring you out of the depths of darkness into the light. Indeed, Allah is Ever Gracious and Most Merciful to you.}

[Surat al-Hadīd: 9]

This is the light by which Allah brings His allies from the darkness of misguidance to the light of guidance. Allah Almighty says:

{Allah is the ally of those who believe; He brings them out from darkness into the light.}

[Surat al-Baqarah: 257]

Allah Almighty also says:

{He is the One Who sends down clear verses to His slave to bring you out of the depths of darkness into the light. Indeed, Allah is Ever Gracious and Most Merciful to you.}

[Surat al-Hadīd: 9]

And it is the light that leads to success in this life and the Hereafter. Allah Almighty says:

{So those who believe in him, they honor and support him, and follow the light which is sent down with him – it is they who will be successful."}

[Surat al-A'rāf: 157]

And it is the light by which a believer walks among people with insight and discernment in life. Allah Almighty says:

{Is the one who was dead and We gave him life [by faith] and gave him a light with which he walks among people like the one in darkness from which he can never escape?}

[Surat al-An'ām: 122]

The guidance of the Qur'an is the light by which the believer crosses the Sirāt (the Bridge over Hellfire that all must pass over) on the Day of Resurrection. Allah Almighty says:

{On the Day when you will see the believing men and the believing women, with their light streaming out ahead of them and to their right…}

[Surat al-Hadīd: 12]

Since the life of this world is full of darkness, my advice to you is to make your way through it with the Light of Allah: the Qur'an. The person who does not have the light from Allah will have no light, and the Qur'an is the Light that illuminates the path of guidance for the allies of Allah.

It Guides to What is Most Righteous

Allah Almighty says: {Surely this Qur'an guides to what is most upright...}[Surat al-Isrā': 9]All of humanity was in confusion (in the pre-Islamic times of Ignorance), with muddled and confused beliefs, religious practices, and morals. They were proceeding without a straight path or a correct methodology to guide and rectify their lives. They were not able, with their limited minds and deviant desires, to attain inner peace and happiness. Therefore, it is from Allah's infinite grace and compassionate concern for mankind that He sent down to them the best of His Scriptures, the Noble Qur'an, to guide them in all aspects of life towards happiness, virtue, peace, security, stability, and prosperity, and to protect them from the evil pathways of immorality and deviancy which only lead them to misery, hardship, and suffering. Allah Almighty says: {O mankind, there has come to you a conclusive proof from your Lord, and We have sent down to you a clear light. As for those who believe in Allah and hold fast to Him, He will admit them into His mercy and grace, and guide them to Himself through a straight path.}[Surat an-Nisā': 174-175]Allah also says:{There has come to you from Allah a light and an evident Book ,through which Allah guides those who seek His pleasure to the ways of peace, and brings them out of the depths of darkness to the light by His Will, and guides them to a straight path.}[Surat al-Mā'idah: 15-16]Whoever desires guidance in his life should ask himself: where is he in respect to the guidance of the Qur'an? He should not waste his time and effort in what does not fulfill his goals; rather he should read and contemplate the Qur'an and learn its guidance to find the truth and the correct direction, as the Jinn said when they listened to the Qur'an, as Allah described:{And [remember] when We sent to you a group of jinn to listen to the Qur'an. When they heard it, they said [to one another], "Listen attentively." Then when it was over, they returned to their people as warners. They said, "O our people, we have heard a scripture that has been sent down after Moses, confirming what came before it; it guides to the truth and to a straight path. OH our people, respond to the one who is calling to Allah, and believe in him; He will forgive you some of your sins and protect you from a painful punishment.}[Surat al-Ahqāf: 29-31]Allah Almighty also says:{Say, "It has been revealed to me that a group of jinn listened [to the Qur'an,] and they said, 'Indeed, we have heard a wondrous recitation that guides to the right way, so we have believed in it, and we will never associate anyone with our Lord.}[Surat al-Jinn: 1-2]The guidance of the Qur'an is complete and perfect without any deviancy. The disaster nowadays is that some Muslims seek guidance from other than the Qur'an, even though Allah has brought them the Qur'an to guide all humanity to that which is best in all ways of life. Whoever seeks guidance from other than the Qur'an will go astray into the worst forms of misguidance.

{Surely this Qur'an guides to what is most upright...}

[Surat al-Isrā': 9]

All of humanity was in confusion (in the pre-Islamic times of Ignorance), with muddled and confused beliefs, religious practices, and morals. They were proceeding without a straight path or a correct methodology to guide and rectify their lives. They were not able, with their limited minds and deviant desires, to attain inner peace and happiness. Therefore, it is from Allah's infinite grace and compassionate concern for mankind that He sent down to them the best of His Scriptures, the Noble Qur'an, to guide them in all aspects of life towards happiness, virtue, peace, security, stability, and prosperity, and to protect them from the evil pathways of immorality and deviancy which only lead them to misery, hardship, and suffering. Allah Almighty says:

{O mankind, there has come to you a conclusive proof from your Lord, and We have sent down to you a clear light.

As for those who believe in Allah and hold fast to Him, He will admit them into His mercy and grace, and guide them to Himself through a straight path.}

[Surat an-Nisā': 174-175]

Allah also says:

{There has come to you from Allah a light and an evident Book.

through which Allah guides those who seek His pleasure to the ways of peace, and brings them out of the depths of darkness to the light by His Will, and guides them to a straight path.}

[Surat al-Mā'idah: 15-16]

Whoever desires guidance in his life should ask himself: where is he in respect to the guidance of the Qur'an?

He should not waste his time and effort in what does not fulfill his goals; rather he should read and contemplate the Qur'an and learn its guidance to find the truth and the correct direction, as the Jinn said when they listened to the Qur'an, as Allah described:

{And [remember] when We sent to you a group of jinn to listen to the Qur'an. When they heard it, they said [to one another], "Listen attentively." Then when it was over, they returned to their people as warners.

They said, "O our people, we have heard a scripture that has been sent down after Moses, confirming what came before it; it guides to the truth and to a straight path.

O our people, respond to the one who is calling to Allah, and believe in him; He will forgive you some of your sins and protect you from a painful punishment.}

[Surat al-Ahqāf: 29-31]

Allah Almighty also says:

{Say, "It has been revealed to me that a group of jinn listened [to the Qur'an,] and they said, 'Indeed, we have heard a wondrous recitation

that guides to the right way, so we have believed in it, and we will never associate anyone with our Lord.}

[Surat al-Jinn: 1-2]

The guidance of the Qur'an is complete and perfect without any deviancy. The disaster nowadays is that some Muslims seek guidance from other than the Qur'an, even though Allah has brought them the Qur'an to guide all humanity to that which is best in all ways of life. Whoever seeks guidance from other than the Qur'an will go astray into the worst forms of misguidance.

He will not go astray nor be miserable

Allah Almighty says:{And whoever follows My guidance will not go astray or be miserable.}[Surat Ta Ha: 123]The merits of the Noble Qur'an are too many to be enumerated in full. It is a great divine grace and favor. Out of Allah's infinite benevolence, He promised many blessings and rewards for those who actively follow its guidance. Among those blessings is the guidance and bliss achieved through the Qur'an and the misguidance and misery it wards off. Allah Almighty says:{And whoever follows My guidance will not go astray or be miserable.}Misguidance and misery go hand in hand, just as their opposites of correct guidance and happiness go hand in hand. The fruit of following guidance is happiness. At-Tabari narrated in his Qur'an exegesis (Tafsīr) that Ibn 'Abbās (may Allah be pleased with him and his father) said: "Whoever reads the Qur'an and follows what is therein will be guided by Allah away from misguidance and saved from the evil accounting on the Day of Reckoning ."Also among the blessings of following it is that it brings safety and joy, which are established in the statement that its follower is safe from fear and grief. Allah Almighty says:{... whoever follows My guidance, there will be no fear for them, nor will they grieve.}[Surat al-Baqarah: 38]Allah Almighty also promised those who follow it a life of abundant provision. Allah Almighty says:{If they had upheld the Torah and the Gospel, and what has been sent down to them from their Lord, they would have been given abundant provisions from above them and from below their feet.}[Surat al-Mā'idah: 66]All of the above constitutes strong motivation to follow the Noble Qur'an, with which Allah wards off every evil from the Muslim and facilitates for him every good thing . Those who refuse to follow it and deny it, reject it, and disbelieve in it, will attain the opposite of those good things promised to its followers. Allah Almighty says:{But whoever turns away from My Reminder will have a miserable life, and on the Day of Resurrection We will raise him blind."}[Surat Ta Ha: 124]This depression is a general distress that they experience in their lives and it ruins life for them no matter what luxuries they are surrounded with. You find them constantly coveting and craving more and feeling panic and anxiety that they would lose what they have or would die and depart this world. This is in addition to what sins and evildoings bring into their heart humiliation, grief, and endless pains. Their life is spent in amassing transient worldly gains, without savoring the pleasure of giving out, which is the real source of joy and happiness in the life of this world. They suffer the distresses of this world that cannot be alleviated except by having faith in Allah, the Lord and Sustainer, and having faith in what is with Allah of immense rewards in the Hereafter. Since their life is as such, Allah Almighty commanded us to turn away from them:{So turn away from whoever turns his back on Our message and desires not except the worldly life.}[Surat an-Najm: 29]No one becomes miserable when they take the Qur'an as companion, because there is no obligation ordained in it that is too hard for them to fulfill. Rather, it is a facilitated legislation that is totally free of hardship and inconvenience, legislated by the Most Merciful in the life of this world and the Hereafter. Allah Almighty says:{And We have certainly made the Qur'an easy for remembrance, so is there anyone who will take heed?}[Surat al-Qamar: 17]Allah also says:{He has chosen you and has not placed upon you in the religion any difficulty}[Surat al-Hajj: 78]Rather, the Qur'an came to remove the oppressive hardship that was imposed on those before us:{ ... and to remove their burdens and the chains that were upon them... }[Surat al-A'rāf: 157]Everything legislated in the Qur'an is easy and in accordance with the natural human disposition. All the commands of Allah therein have complete or predominant benefit, and all of His prohibitions protect from complete or predominant harm. There is not a single ordinance in the Qur'an that is beyond human capability or that incurs hardship and suffering. Allah Almighty says:{We have not sent down the Qur'an to you [O Prophet] to cause you distress}[Surat Ta Ha: 2]At-Tabari narrated in his Qur'an exegesis (Tafsīr) that Qatādah said: "No, by Allah, He did not make it a source of distress, but He made it a mercy and light, and a guide to Paradise. "How can an intelligent person distance himself from the source of happiness and bliss for himself and his community?

{And whoever follows My guidance will not go astray or be miserable.}

[Surat Ta Ha: 123]

The merits of the Noble Qur'an are too many to be enumerated in full. It is a great divine grace and favor. Out of Allah's infinite benevolence, He promised many blessings and rewards for those who actively follow its guidance. Among those blessings is the guidance and bliss achieved through the Qur'an and the misguidance and misery it wards off. Allah Almighty says:

{And whoever follows My guidance will not go astray or be miserable.}

Misguidance and misery go hand in hand, just as their opposites of correct guidance and happiness go hand in hand. The fruit of following guidance is happiness. At-Tabari narrated in his Qur'an exegesis (Tafsīr) that Ibn 'Abbās (may Allah be pleased with him and his father) said:

"Whoever reads the Qur'an and follows what is therein will be guided by Allah away from misguidance and saved from the evil accounting on the Day of Reckoning."

Also among the blessings of following it is that it brings safety and joy, which are established in the statement that its follower is safe from fear and grief. Allah Almighty says:

{... whoever follows My guidance, there will be no fear for them, nor will they grieve.}

[Surat al-Baqarah: 38]

Allah Almighty also promised those who follow it a life of abundant provision. Allah Almighty says:

{If they had upheld the Torah and the Gospel, and what has been sent down to them from their Lord, they would have been given abundant provisions from above them and from below their feet.}

[Surat al-Mā'idah: 66]

All of the above constitutes strong motivation to follow the Noble Qur'an, with which Allah wards off every evil from the Muslim and facilitates for him every good thing.

Those who refuse to follow it and deny it, reject it, and disbelieve in it, will attain the opposite of those good things promised to its followers. Allah Almighty says:

{But whoever turns away from My Reminder will have a miserable life, and on the Day of Resurrection We will raise him blind."}

[Surat Ta Ha: 124]

This depression is a general distress that they experience in their lives and it ruins life for them no matter what luxuries they are surrounded with. You find them constantly coveting and craving more and feeling panic and anxiety that they would lose what they have or would die and depart this world. This is in addition to what sins and evildoings bring into their heart humiliation, grief, and endless pains.

Their life is spent in amassing transient worldly gains, without savoring the pleasure of giving out, which is the real source of joy and happiness in the life of this world. They suffer the distresses of this world that cannot be alleviated except by having faith in Allah, the Lord and Sustainer, and having faith in what is with Allah of immense rewards in the Hereafter. Since their life is as such, Allah Almighty commanded us to turn away from them:

{So turn away from whoever turns his back on Our message and desires not except the worldly life.}

[Surat an-Najm: 29]

No one becomes miserable when they take the Qur'an as companion, because there is no obligation ordained in it that is too hard for them to fulfill. Rather, it is a facilitated legislation that is totally free of hardship and inconvenience, legislated by the Most Merciful in the life of this world and the Hereafter. Allah Almighty says:

{And We have certainly made the Qur'an easy for remembrance, so is there anyone who will take heed?}

[Surat al-Qamar: 17]

Allah also says:

{He has chosen you and has not placed upon you in the religion any difficulty}

[Surat al-Hajj: 78]

Rather, the Qur'an came to remove the oppressive hardship that was imposed on those before us:

{ ... and to remove their burdens and the chains that were upon them... }

[Surat al-A'rāf: 157]

Everything legislated in the Qur'an is easy and in accordance with the natural human disposition. All the commands of Allah therein have completed or predominant benefit, and all of His prohibitions protect from complete or predominant harm. There is not a single ordinance in the Qur'an that is beyond human capability or that incurs hardship and suffering. Allah Almighty says:

{We have not sent down the Qur'an to you [O Prophet] to cause you distress}

[Surat Ta Ha: 2]

At-Tabari narrated in his Qur'an exegesis (Tafsīr) that Qatādah said:

"No, by Allah, He did not make it a source of distress, but He made it a mercy and light, and a guide to Paradise."

How can an intelligent person distance himself from the source of happiness and bliss for himself and his community?

Healing and Mercy

Allah Almighty says:

{And We send down of the Qur'an that which is healing and mercy for the believers.}

[Surat al-Isrā': 82]

Allah Almighty gave many descriptions to the Qur'an that make its merit clear to His servants and encourage them to embrace it. Among these descriptions is that the Qur'an is a healing; a healing for both physical and spiritual ailments. Therefore, scholars classified this healing into into two kinds:

The first: a healing for what is in the chests :Allah Almighty stated this explicitly, because the chest (which houses the heart) is the abode of faith and guidance, and it is what directs the senses and body parts towards action. The righteousness of the heart leads to the righteousness of words and deeds, and vice versa. Allah Almighty says:{O mankind, there has come to you instruction from your Lord, and a healing for what is in the chests, and a guidance and mercy for the believers.}[Surat Yūnus: 57]The Qur'an is the healing for the diseases of the heart: disbelief, idolatry, and hypocrisy, and all corrupt ideological or sectarian beliefs and wicked lusts that prevent a person from accepting the truth and yielding to it. The Qur'an is a healing for doubts and suspicions that hinder from accepting the true knowledge, and is a healing for deviating blindness and false ideologies. The Qur'an is a healing for what hearts harbor of arrogance, rancor, hatred, and envy, all of which create enmity and evil behavior. It is also a healing for whispering of Satan and all kinds of diseases that affect the heart. The second: a healing for the diseases of the body: The scholars derived this merit of the Qur'an from the general indication of the verse as Allah Almighty says: {Say, "It is a guidance and healing for those who believe. As for those who do not believe, there is deafness in their ears and they are blind to [understand] it}[Surat Fussilat: 44]They also cited the authentic Prophetic narrations wherein the Prophet (may Allah's peace and blessings be upon him) sought healing for his ailments by the Qur'an.One example is the narration by Al-Bukhārī where 'Ā'ishah (may Allah be pleased with her) told 'Urwah: "Whenever the Messenger of Allah (may Allah's peace and blessings be upon him) became ill, he used to recite the Mu'awwidhāt (the last two [or three] chapters of the Qur'an) and blow his breath over himself and rub his hands over his body. Therefore, when he was afflicted with his final illness in which he died, I started reciting the Mu'awwidhāt and blow my breath over him as he used to do, and then I rubbed his hand over his body . "He also approved it when his Companions recited verses from the Qur'an (Surat al-Fātihah) to treat a tribal chief who had received a poisonous sting and fell gravely ill. The man was cured, so the tribesmen gave the Companions a herd of sheep as a reward. When this incident was related to the Prophet (may Allah's peace and blessings be upon him), he smiled and said to them:"And how do you know that it is a Ruqyah (a recitation that heals)? You were correct. Divide the reward (amongst yourselves) and allocate a share for me." And how many times have we seen sicknesses and pains which the physicians were unable to treat but were cured by the healing power of the blessed recitation of the Qur'an. But we must know that the precondition for seeking healing in the Qur'an is to have strong belief in it, and to believe in what Allah says about it, and to proceed to use it as a means of healing with certitude and conviction. Can an illness have any effect when it is confronted with the words of the Lord and Sovereign of the heavens and the earth? This is why the verse specifically stated that it is a cure for the believers. As to those who turn away from it, it only increases their loss:{And We send down of the Qur'an that which is healing and mercy for the believers, but it does not increase the wrongdoers except in loss.}[Surat al-Isrā': 82]Note that Allah Almighty described the Qur'an as healing and not as medicine, so that we believe with certainty in its general healing power, because medicine may heal or may not. Rather, we should know that there is no cure as complete and perfect as the Qur'an for all our physical and spiritual illnesses. Seeking a cure for our social, political, economic, psychological, and all other diseases in other than the Qur'an will only increase our sickness. The fall of the western theories and their successive failure proves this truth about the Qur'an. How can we be heedless of a Book that Allah Almighty described as 'healing'? Then he followed that with describing it as 'mercy', because it denotes perfect care and concern for all that is good. There is no disease or ailment but that the Qur'an clarifies for you what it is, its symptoms, causes, and consequences, and then describes how to cure it in the best and most perfect manner that leads to complete healing in a way not found in any other source.

Allah Almighty stated this explicitly, because the chest (which houses the heart) is the abode of faith and guidance, and it is what directs the senses and body parts towards action. The righteousness of the heart leads to the righteousness of words and deeds, and vice versa. Allah Almighty says:

{O mankind, there has come to you instruction from your Lord, and a healing for what is in the chests, and a guidance and mercy for the believers.}

[Surat Yūnus: 57]

The Qur'an is the healing for the diseases of the heart: disbelief, idolatry, and hypocrisy, and all corrupt ideological or sectarian beliefs and wicked lusts that prevent a person from accepting the truth and yielding to it. The Qur'an is a healing for doubts and suspicions that hinder from accepting the true knowledge, and is a healing for deviating blindness and false ideologies. The Qur'an is a healing for what hearts harbor of arrogance, rancor, hatred, and envy, all of which create enmity and evil behavior. It is also a healing for whispering of Satan and all kinds of diseases that affect the heart.

The second: a healing for the diseases of the body:

The scholars derived this merit of the Qur'an from the general indication of the verse as Allah Almighty says:

{Say, "It is a guidance and healing for those who believe. As for those who do not believe, there is deafness in their ears and they are blind to [understand] it}

[Surat Fussilat: 44]

They also cited the authentic Prophetic narrations wherein the Prophet (may Allah's peace and blessings be upon him) sought healing for his ailments by the Qur'an.

One example is the narration by Al-Bukhāri where 'Ā'ishah (may Allah be pleased with her) told 'Urwah: "Whenever the Messenger of Allah (may Allah's peace and blessings be upon him) became ill, he used to recite the Mu'awwidhāt (the last two [or three] chapters of the Qur'an) and blow his breath over himself and rub his hands over his body. Therefore, when he was afflicted with his final illness in which he died, I started reciting the Mu'awwidhāt and blow my breath over him as he used to do, and then I rubbed his hand over his body."

He also approved it when his Companions recited verses from the Qur'an (Surat al-Fātihah) to treat a tribal chief who had received a poisonous sting and fell gravely ill. The man was cured, so the tribesmen gave the Companions a herd of sheep as a reward. When this incident was related to the Prophet (may Allah's peace and blessings be upon him), he smiled and said to them:

"And how do you know that it is a Ruqyah (a recitation that heals)? You were correct. Divide the reward (amongst yourselves) and allocate a share for me."

And how many times have we seen sicknesses and pains which the physicians were unable to treat but were cured by the healing power of the blessed recitation of the Qur'an. But we must know that the precondition for seeking healing in the Qur'an is to have strong belief in it, and to believe in what Allah says about it, and to proceed to use it as a means of healing with certitude and conviction. Can an illness have any effect when it is confronted with the words of the Lord and Sovereign of the heavens and the earth?

This is why the verse specifically stated that it is a cure for the believers. As to those who turn away from it, it only increases their loss:

{And We send down of the Qur'an that which is healing and mercy for the believers, but it does not increase the wrongdoers except in loss.}

[Surat al-Isrā': 82]

Note that Allah Almighty described the Qur'an as healing and not as medicine, so that we believe with certainty in its general healing power, because medicine may heal or may not. Rather, we should know that there is no cure as complete and perfect as the Qur'an for all our physical and spiritual illnesses. Seeking a cure for our social, political, economic, psychological, and all other diseases in other than the Qur'an will only increase our sickness. The fall of the western theories and their successive failure proves this truth about the Qur'an. How can we be heedless of a Book that Allah Almighty described as 'healing'?

Then he followed that with describing it as 'mercy', because it denotes perfect care and concern for all that is good. There is no disease or ailment but that the Qur'an clarifies for you what it is, its symptoms, causes, and consequences, and then describes how to cure it in the best and most perfect manner that leads to complete healing in a way not found in any other source.

A Trade that will never fail

Allah Almighty says:{Indeed, those who recite the Book of Allah and establish prayer and spend [in His cause] out of what We have provided them, secretly and publicly, hoping for a trade that will never fail.}[Surat Fātir: 29]Actively living with the Qur'an, by listening to it, reciting it, memorizing it, learning and teaching it, and most of all, by acting according to its guidance, is indeed a profitable business and a great gain. Merit and goodness are for those who hope for this trade and work for it. It was narrated by Al-Bukhāri, on the authority of 'Uthmān (may Allah be pleased with him) that the Prophet (may Allah's peace and blessings be upon him) said: "The best of you are those who learn the Qur'an and teach it. "In another narration, he said :"Verily, the most meritorious of you are those who learn the Qur'an and teach it. "There are many textual proofs that detail the numerous ways of profiting through the Qur'an, including: First: listening to it; it yields mercy, guidance, and increase in faith. Al-Qurtubi mentioned in his Tafsīr (exegesis) that Al-Layth said :"It is said that mercy does not reach anyone faster than it reaches the one who listens to the Qur'an, because Allah Almighty says:{When the Qur'an is recited, listen to it and pay attention, so that you may receive mercy.}[Surat al-A'rāf: 204]Allah Almighty also says:{... so give glad tiding to My worshipers, those who listen to the speech and follow the best of it. Those are the ones whom Allah has guided, and those are the people of understanding.}[Surat az-Zumar: 17-18]Allah Almighty also says:{The true believers are those whose hearts are filled with awe when Allah is mentioned, and their faith increases when His verses are recited to them, and they put their trust only in their Lord}[Surat al-Anfāl: 2]Second: reciting it; it yields a great reward. Allah Almighty says:{Those who recite the Book of Allah, establish prayer, and spend out of what We have provided for them, secretly and openly, hoping for a deal that will suffer no loss,

so that He will reward them in full and give them more out of His bounty. He is All-Forgiving, Most Appreciative.}[Surat Fātir: 29-30]How could it not be a profitable transaction when Allah has decreed that reciting one letter yields ten units of reward?!Imam Muslim narrated on the authority of 'Uqbah ibn 'Āmir (may Allah be pleased with him) that he said: The Prophet (may Allah's peace and blessing be upon him) came out while we were at the Suffah (an area at the back of the Prophet's Mosque in Madīnah) and said: "Which of you would like to go out every morning to But-hān or Al-'Aqīq and bring therefrom two large she-camels without committing sin or severing the ties of kinship ? "We said, "O Messenger of Allah, we would love that." He said: "Does not one of you go out in the morning to the mosque and learn or recite two verses from the Book of Allah Almighty is better for him than two she-camels, and three (verses) are better for him than three (camels), and four (verses) are better for him than four (camels), and from their number in camels." Third: studying it with others; tranquility and mercy descend upon those studying it. Imam Muslim narrated on the authority of Abu Hurairah (may Allah be pleased with him) that the Prophet (may Allah's peace and blessings be upon him) said:"... and whoever follows a path to seek knowledge, Allah will make easy for him a path to Paradise. No people gather together in one of the houses of Allah (mosques), reciting the Book of Allah, and studying it among themselves except that tranquility descends upon them, mercy envelops them, the angels surround them, and Allah mentions them amongst those who are with Him. Whoever is slowed down by his deeds will not be hastened forward by his lineage. "Fourth: the person skilled with the Qur'an; he is with the noble righteous scribes of the angels, whether he is skilled in reciting it or in memorizing it. Imam Muslim narrated that the Prophet (may Allah's peace and blessings be upon him) said: "The one who reads the Qur'an skillfully will be in the company of the noble righteous scribes of the angels, and the one who reads the Qur'an but stutters and finds it difficult receives a double reward. "The one skilled in memorizing it is mentioned in a narration by Imam Al-Bukhāri wherein the Prophet (may Allah's peace and blessings be upon him) said: "The person who recites the Qur'an while he knows it by heart is with the noble righteous scribes of the angels. And the person who recites it while trying to memorize it and he finds it difficult will have a double reward. "Fifth: acting upon it; acting according to the Qur'an is the reason for success in the life of this world and in the Hereafter. Allah Almighty says:{So those who believe in him, they honor and support him, and follow the light which is sent down with him – it is they who will be successful."}[Surat al-A'rāf: 157]Imam Muslim narrated that the Prophet (may Allah's peace and blessings be upon him) said: "On the Day of Resurrection, the Qur'an and those who acted according to it will be brought with Surat al-Baqarah and Surat Āl 'Imran preceding them."

{Indeed, those who recite the Book of Allah and establish prayer and spend [in His cause] out of what We have provided them, secretly and publicly, hoping for a trade that will never fail.}

[Surat Fātir: 29]

Actively living with the Qur'an, by listening to it, reciting it, memorizing it, learning and teaching it, and most of all, by acting according to its guidance, is indeed a profitable business and a great gain. Merit and goodness are for those who hope for this trade and work for it. It was narrated by Al-Bukhāri, on the authority of 'Uthmān (may Allah be pleased with him) that the Prophet (may Allah's peace and blessings be upon him) said:

"The best of you are those who learn the Qur'an and teach it."

In another narration, he said:

"Verily, the most meritorious of you are those who learn the Qur'an and teach it."

There are many textual proofs that detail the numerous ways of profiting through the Qur'an, including:

First: listening to it; it yields mercy, guidance, and increase in faith. Al-Qurtubi mentioned in his Tafsīr (exegesis) that Al-Layth said:

"It is said that mercy does not reach anyone faster than it reaches the one who listens to the Qur'an, because Allah Almighty says:

{When the Qur'an is recited, listen to it and pay attention, so that you may receive mercy.}

[Surat al-A'rāf: 204]

Allah Almighty also says:

{... so give glad tiding to My worshipers,

those who listen to the speech and follow the best of it. Those are the ones whom Allah has guided, and those are the people of understanding.}

[Surat az-Zumar: 17-18]

Allah Almighty also says:

{The true believers are those whose hearts are filled with awe when Allah is mentioned, and their faith increases when His verses are recited to them, and they put their trust only in their Lord}

[Surat al-Anfāl: 2]

Second: reciting it; it yields a great reward. Allah Almighty says:

{Those who recite the Book of Allah, establish prayer, and spend out of what We have provided for them, secretly and openly, hoping for a deal that will suffer no loss,

so that He will reward them in full and give them more out of His bounty. He is All-Forgiving, Most Appreciative.}

[Surat Fātir: 29-30]

How could it not be a profitable transaction when Allah has decreed that reciting one letter yields ten units of reward?!

Imam Muslim narrated on the authority of 'Uqbah ibn 'Āmir (may Allah be pleased with him) that he said: The Prophet (may Allah's peace and blessing be upon him) came out while we were at the Suffah (an area at the back of the Prophet's Mosque in Madīnah) and said:

"Which of you would like to go out every morning to But-hān or Al-'Aqīq and bring therefrom two large she-camels without committing sin or severing the ties of kinship?"

We said, "O Messenger of Allah, we would love that." He said:

"Does not one of you go out in the morning to the mosque and learn or recite two verses from the Book of Allah Almighty is better for him than two she-camels, and three (verses) are better for him than three (camels), and four (verses) are better for him than four (camels), and from their number in camels."

Third: studying it with others; tranquility and mercy descend upon those studying it. Imam Muslim narrated on the authority of Abu Hurairah (may Allah be pleased with him) that the Prophet (may Allah's peace and blessings be upon him) said:

"... and whoever follows a path to seek knowledge, Allah will make easy for him a path to Paradise. No people gather together in one of the houses of Allah (mosques), reciting the Book of Allah, and studying it among themselves except that tranquility descends upon them, mercy envelops them, the angels surround them, and Allah mentions them amongst those who are with Him. Whoever is slowed down by his deeds will not be hastened forward by his lineage."

Fourth: the person skilled with the Qur'an; he is with the noble righteous scribes of the angels, whether he is skilled in reciting it or in memorizing it. Imam Muslim narrated that the Prophet (may Allah's peace and blessings be upon him) said:

"The one who reads the Qur'an skillfully will be in the company of the noble righteous scribes of the angels, and the one who reads the Qur'an but stutters and finds it difficult receives a double reward."

The one skilled in memorizing it is mentioned in a narration by Imam Al-Bukhāri wherein the Prophet (may Allah's peace and blessings be upon him) said:

"The person who recites the Qur'an while he knows it by heart is with the noble righteous scribes of the angels. And the person who recites it while trying to memorize it and he finds it difficult will have a double reward."

Fifth: acting upon it; acting according to the Qur'an is the reason for success in the life of this world and in the Hereafter. Allah Almighty says:

{So those who believe in him, they honor and support him, and follow the light which is sent down with him – it is they who will be successful."}

[Surat al-A'rāf: 157]

Imam Muslim narrated that the Prophet (may Allah's peace and blessings be upon him) said:

"On the Day of Resurrection, the Qur'an and those who acted according to it will be brought with Surat al-Baqarah and Surat Āl 'Imrān preceding them."

A Rope of Rescue for the one who holds on to it

Allah Almighty says: {And hold fast to the rope of Allah all together and do not become divided... }[Surat Āl 'Imrān: 103]

{And hold fast to the rope of Allah all together and do not become divided... }

[Surat Āl 'Imrān: 103]

Every person faces various dangers in life, and therefore he seeks means of rescue for himself and those around him. Allah Almighty commanded us in the Qur'an to hold fast to two means of rescue whereby we would be saved. They are:

First: Holding fast to Allah, as He says: {And hold fast to Allah. He is your protector; and excellent is the protector, and excellent is the helper.}[Surat al-Hajj: 78]This is achieved by devoting worship sincerely to Him and relying on Him alone without any partner unto Him. Second: Holding fast to His Book. Allah Almighty says: {O mankind, there has come to you a conclusive proof from your Lord, and We have sent down to you a clear light. So those who believe in Allah and hold fast to it [the Qur'an] – He will admit them to mercy and bounty from Himself, and guide them to Himself on a straight path.}[Surat an-

Nisā': 174, 175]Imam Muslim narrated that the Prophet (may Allah's peace and blessings be upon him) said: "Behold, for I am leaving among you two weighty things, one of which is the Book of Allah, the Exalted and Glorious. It is the rope of Allah... He who follows it will be upon right guidance and he who abandons it will be in error... "

{And hold fast to Allah. He is your protector; and excellent is the protector, and excellent is the helper.}

[Surat al-Hajj: 78]

This is achieved by devoting worship sincerely to Him and relying on Him alone without any partner unto Him.

Second: Holding fast to His Book. Allah Almighty says:

{O mankind, there has come to you a conclusive proof from your Lord, and We have sent down to you a clear light.

So those who believe in Allah and hold fast to it [the Qur'an] – He will admit them to mercy and bounty from Himself, and guide them to Himself on a straight path.}

[Surat an-Nisā': 174, 175]

Imam Muslim narrated that the Prophet (may Allah's peace and blessings be upon him) said:

"Behold, for I am leaving among you two weighty things, one of which is the Book of Allah, the Exalted and Glorious. It is the rope of Allah... He who follows it will be upon right guidance and he who abandons it will be in error... "

Holding fast to the rope of Allah (the Qur'an) protects the holder from misguidance and destruction and all the pathways leading to loss and failure. It sets him on the path of security and guidance. The Qur'an is a protection for those who seek protection in it and a rescue rope for those who follow it, because it is the firm bond that will never break for those who hold on firmly to it. As the Arab poet said:

O my people, the Qur'an is the rope of our salvation,

So hold fast to it lest we drown,

Let our divided groups gather around the Book,

So that we will not fight each other nor be separated,

Let us make it the judge in all our affairs,

And be certain that the promise of Allah will come true.

Holding fast to it is achieved by making it the sole methodology of our life apart from any opinions and desires of men. It is a necessity for our deliverance from misguidance, for attaining happiness in the life of this world, and for our salvation on the Day of Judgment. How can a rational person not hold firm to what his salvation lies within? There is no salvation in other than the Qur'an. It is the Book that commands for us all that is good, prohibits all that is evil, establishes all truth and justice, invalidates all falsehood, guides to all good deeds, and forbids all evil deeds. By this Book, Allah brought the hearts together after He unified by it the beliefs of the Muslim nation and its ideology and perspective on life.

There is no salvation in other than the Qur'an. It is the Book that commands for us all that is good, prohibits all that is evil, establishes all truth and justice, invalidates all falsehood, guides to all good deeds, and forbids all evil deeds. By this Book, Allah brought the hearts together after He unified by it the beliefs of the Muslim nation and its ideology and perspective on life.

It is imperative for the believer to realize that his religion lies entirely in holding fast to Allah and His rope, in terms of knowledge, actions, devotion, and seeking aid, and by doing this diligently and steadfastly until the Day of Resurrection.

A Book wherein you are mentioned

Allah Almighty says:{We have certainly sent down to you a Book in which is your mention. Then will you not reason?}[Surat al-Anbiyā': 10]Among the greatest matters that urge us to believe in the Noble Qur'an and to learn it, teach it, act upon it, and hold fast onto it, are the words of Allah Almighty:{We have certainly sent down to you a Book in which is your mention}Your mention means: your dignity, honor, and power. This verse clarifies that if the nation believed in the Qur'an and followed its guidance, it would rise in status and honor among all the nations of the world. How could this not be when it is the noblest Scripture that Allah has revealed? Allah Almighty says: {Sād. By the Qur'an, full of reminder,}[Sād: 1]Meaning: of great status, nobility, and honor. Its noble status was evident in the nation of the Arabs at the time of its revelation. Contemplate how it transformed it from a nation of hostility and disintegration to a nation of unity, mercy, and honor. That nation eventually reigned the peoples through its knowledge and civilization that emanated from the wise guidance of the Qur'an. Allah Almighty reminds of this when He says:{Remember the favor of Allah upon you when you were enemies, then He reconciled your hearts, making you brethren by His grace. And you were on the brink of a fiery pit and He delivered you from it. This is how Allah makes His verses clear to you, so that you may be guided.}[Surat Āl 'Imrān: 103] Throughout the history of the Muslim nation, the fruit of adhering to the Qur'an was glory and honor, and the fruit of neglecting it was humiliation, degradation, and weakness. Because heedlessness of the importance of the Qur'an reflects lack of reason and awareness, Allah Almighty concludes the verse that explains this with the question: {Then will you not reason?} in order to highlight the ugliness of their turning away from the Qur'an. Since the Qur'an is a source of honor to one who follows it and acts according to its guidance, for it contains sublime beliefs, noble morals, and the best of deeds that elevate whoever adheres to them, Allah commanded His Messenger and the Muslim nation which follows him, saying: {So adhere to that which is revealed to you. Indeed, you are on a straight path. And indeed, it is a remembrance for you and your people, and you [all] are going to be questioned.}[Surat az-Zukhruf: 43, 44]It is reprehensible that a Muslim who has knowledge does not give due care to this Book that is the source of honor and dignity for him and his nation. Therefore, the Qur'an is the refuge and sanctuary for every Muslim who has knowledge. He exerts himself and spends his most precious possessions to learn it, teach it, advise people to adhere to it, and spread its guidance. These acts are part of acknowledging this blessing and expressing gratitude for it.{... and remember Allah's Blessing upon you, and what He sent down to you of the Book and Wisdom, exhorting you thereby... }[Surat al-Baqarah: 231]

{We have certainly sent down to you a Book in which is your mention. Then will you not reason?}

[Surat al-Anbiyā': 10]

Among the greatest matters that urge us to believe in the Noble Qur'an and to learn it, teach it, act upon it, and hold fast onto it, are the words of Allah Almighty:

{We have certainly sent down to you a Book in which is your mention}

Your mention means: your dignity, honor, and power. This verse clarifies that if the nation believed in the Qur'an and followed its guidance, it would rise in status and honor among all the nations of the world. How could this not be when it is the noblest Scripture that Allah has revealed?

Allah Almighty says:

{Sād. By the Qur'an, full of reminder,}

[Sād: 1]

Meaning: of great status, nobility, and honor.

Its noble status was evident in the nation of the Arabs at the time of its revelation. Contemplate how it transformed it from a nation of hostility and disintegration to a nation of unity, mercy, and honor.

That nation eventually reigned the peoples through its knowledge and civilization that emanated from the wise guidance of the Qur'an. Allah Almighty reminds of this when He says:

{Remember the favor of Allah upon you when you were enemies, then He reconciled your hearts, making you brethren by His grace. And you were on the brink of a fiery pit and He delivered you from it. This is how Allah makes His verses clear to you, so that you may be guided.}

[Surat Āl 'Imrān: 103] Throughout the history of the Muslim nation, the fruit of adhering to the Qur'an was glory and honor, and the fruit of neglecting it was humiliation, degradation, and weakness. Because heedlessness of the importance of the Qur'an reflects lack of reason and awareness, Allah Almighty concludes the verse that explains this with the question: {Then will you not reason?} in order to highlight the ugliness of their turning away from the Qur'an.

Since the Qur'an is a source of honor to one who follows it and acts according to its guidance, for it contains sublime beliefs, noble morals, and the best of deeds that elevate whoever adheres to them, Allah commanded His Messenger and the Muslim nation which follows him, saying:

{So adhere to that which is revealed to you. Indeed, you are on a straight path.

And indeed, it is a remembrance for you and your people, and you [all] are going to be questioned.}

[Surat az-Zukhruf: 43, 44]

It is reprehensible that a Muslim who has knowledge does not give due care to this Book that is the source of honor and dignity for him and his nation.

Therefore, the Qur'an is the refuge and sanctuary for every Muslim who has knowledge. He exerts himself and spends his most precious possessions to learn it, teach it, advise people to adhere to it, and spread its guidance. These acts are part of acknowledging this blessing and expressing gratitude for it.

{... and remember Allah's Blessing upon you, and what He sent down to you of the Book and Wisdom, exhorting you thereby... }

[Surat al-Baqarah: 231]

The Intercessor Whose Intercession is Accepted

Allah Almighty says:{Then We made to inherit the Book those whom We have chosen from among Our slaves. But among them are some who wrong themselves, some follow a middle course, and some are foremost in good deeds with Allah's permission. That is the great bountyThey will enter gardens of perpetual residence; they will be adorned therein with bracelets of gold and pearls, and their garments will be of silk.}[Surat Fātir: 32, 33]There will be great distress and grief on the Day of Resurrection, since everyone will be seeking his own way to safety and salvation. From among the abundant virtues and merits of the Qur'an that will become evident on that momentous Day is that the companions of the Qur'an will be singled out with honor and distinction. It is established by many irrefutable proofs that the Qur'an will be an intercessor and advocate for those who took it as their companion by reciting it, reflecting upon it, and acting according to it; for those that made the Qur'an an important part of their life, even if they did themselves injustice (by sinning) or were moderate (not foremost in doing good). The Qur'an will intercede for them until they are granted entry into Paradise. Imam Muslim narrated that Abu Umāmah al-Bāhili (may Allah be pleased with him) said: I heard the Messenger of Allah (may Allah's peace and blessings be upon him) say: "Recite the Qur'an, for on the Day of Resurrection it will come as an intercessor for those who recite It. Recite the two bright ones, (Surat) al-Baqarah and (Surat) Āl 'Imrān, for on the Day of Resurrection they will come as two clouds or two shades, or two flocks of birds in ranks, pleading for those who recite them. Recite Surat al-Baqarah, for to take recourse to it is a blessing and to give it up is a cause of grief, and the sorcerers cannot confront it."Imam Ahmad and others narrated that 'Abdullah ibn 'Amr (may Allah be pleased with him and his father) reported that he heard the Messenger of Allah (may Allah's peace and blessings be upon him) say: "Fasting and the Qur'an intercede for the slave on the Day of Judgment. Fasting will say, 'O my Lord, I kept him away from his food and his lusts by day, so accept my intercession for him.' The Qur'an will say, 'I kept him away from sleep by night, so accept my intercession for him.' He said: 'Then their intersession with be accepted.' "And even a single Surah (chapter) will intercede for the person who consistently reads it, as authentically narrated by Abu Dāwūd, at-Tirmidhi, an-Nasā'i, Ibn Mājah, and others, that the Messenger of Allah (may Allah's peace and blessings be upon him) said: "Indeed, there is a Surah in the Qur'an of thirty verses that interceded for a man until he was forgiven. It is {Tabārak alladhi biyadih-il-mulk} (i.e. Surat al-Mulk)."It was narrated on the authority of Ibn Mas'ūd (may Allah be pleased with him) that he said: "The Qur'an is an intercessor whose intercession is accepted, and an opponent whose testimony is trusted. Whoever puts it in front of him, it will lead him to Paradise, and whoever puts it behind his back, it will drive him to Hell."

{Then We made to inherit the Book those whom We have chosen from among Our slaves. But among them are some who wrong themselves, some follow a middle course, and some are foremost in good deeds with Allah's permission. That is the great bounty

They will enter gardens of perpetual residence; they will be adorned therein with bracelets of gold and pearls, and their garments will be of silk.}

[Surat Fātir: 32, 33]

There will be great distress and grief on the Day of Resurrection, since everyone will be seeking his own way to safety and salvation. From among the abundant virtues and merits of the Qur'an that will become evident on that momentous Day is that the companions of the Qur'an will be singled out with honor and distinction. It is established by many irrefutable proofs that the Qur'an will be an intercessor and advocate for those who took it as their companion by reciting it, reflecting upon it, and acting according to it; for those that made the Qur'an an important part of their life, even if they did themselves injustice (by sinning) or were moderate (not foremost in doing good). The Qur'an will intercede for them until they are granted entry into Paradise.

Imam Muslim narrated that Abu Umāmah al-Bāhili (may Allah be pleased with him) said: I heard the Messenger of Allah (may Allah's peace and blessings be upon him) say:

"Recite the Qur'an, for on the Day of Resurrection it will come as an intercessor for those who recite It. Recite the two bright ones, (Surat) al-Baqarah and (Surat) Āl 'Imrān, for on the Day of Resurrection they will come as two clouds or two shades, or two flocks of birds in ranks, pleading for those who recite them. Recite Surat al-Baqarah, for to take recourse to it is a blessing and to give it up is a cause of grief, and the sorcerers cannot confront it."

Imam Ahmad and others narrated that 'Abdullah ibn 'Amr (may Allah be pleased with him and his father) reported that he heard the Messenger of Allah (may Allah's peace and blessings be upon him) say:

"Fasting and the Qur'an intercede for the slave on the Day of Judgment. Fasting will say, 'O my Lord, I kept him away from his food and his lusts by day, so accept my intercession for him.' The Qur'an will say, 'I kept him away from sleep by night, so accept my intercession for him.' He said: 'Then their intersession with be accepted.'"

And even a single Surah (chapter) will intercede for the person who consistently reads it, as authentically narrated by Abu Dāwūd, at-Tirmidhi, an-Nasā'i, Ibn Mājah, and others, that the Messenger of Allah (may Allah's peace and blessings be upon him) said:

"Indeed, there is a Surah in the Qur'an of thirty verses that interceded for a man until he was forgiven. It is {Tabārak alladhi biyadih-il-mulk} (i.e. Surat al-Mulk)."

It was narrated on the authority of Ibn Mas'ūd (may Allah be pleased with him) that he said:

"The Qur'an is an intercessor whose intercession is accepted, and an opponent whose testimony is trusted. Whoever puts it in front of him, it will lead him to Paradise, and whoever puts it behind his back, it will drive him to Hell."

Imam ash-Shātibi said in his famous poem on Qur'anic recitations:

The Book of Allah is the trustiest intercessor,

And the richest recital giving blessings,

It is the best companion whose conversation never wearies,

And his recitation of it increases his beauty,

If this person is wondering within the shades of darkness,

In his grave, He will find it a bright light rejoicing,

There it will congratulate him with a resting place and garden,

And because of it the pinnacle of status will be revealed to him.

Whoever comes to realize this fact of faith, realizes the great virtue of the Qur'an and the honor of taking it as his companion in life. He realizes that his life with the Qur'an is success in this life and in the Hereafter.

Whoever realizes all these merits and virtues of the Qur'an that we have mentioned and others, will come to know that if a person can do without the water that gives him life, he cannot do without the words of Allah that sustain his true life and his salvation in this world and in the Hereafter. He would know that Allah has given him the most abundant wealth and the ultimate sufficiency in life. For this reason, Allah addresses His Messenger saying:{We have surely given you the seven oft-repeated verses and the great Qur'an. Do not look longingly at the pleasures We have given certain classes of them, nor grieve over them, but lower your wing [in humility] to the believers.}[Surat al-Hijr: 87-88]Every blessing, no matter how great, is small and insignificant compared to the Qur'an. In order to realize its merit, it is sufficient to know that the Qur'an is your guide to the happiest states, the greatest honors, and the highest ranks and stations.

For this reason, Allah addresses His Messenger saying:

{We have surely given you the seven oft-repeated verses and the great Qur'an.

Do not look longingly at the pleasures We have given certain classes of them, nor grieve over them, but lower your wing [in humility] to the believers.}

[Surat al-Hijr: 87-88]

Every blessing, no matter how great, is small and insignificant compared to the Qur'an. In order to realize its merit, it is sufficient to know that the Qur'an is your guide to the happiest states, the greatest honors, and the highest ranks and stations.

In conclusion, I say that my people have abandoned this Qur'an.

Allah Almighty says:{The Messenger said, "O my Lord, my people have taken this Qur'an as a thing to be abandoned."}[Surat al-Furqān: 30]

{The Messenger said, "O my Lord, my people have taken this Qur'an as a thing to be abandoned."}

[Surat al-Furqān: 30]

After this brief journey of faith and knowledge about the greatness and magnificence of the Qur'an and its beauty, merits, status, and the supreme importance for the believer in particular to live in its shades, we say in the conclusion of this treatise:

The most devastating loss lies in turning away from the words of Allah, the Lord Sovereign and Creator of the universe. Allah Almighty says:{Who does greater wrong than one who is reminded of the verses of his Lord, then turns away from them? We will surely take vengeance upon the wicked.}[Surat as-Sajdah: 22]Or in forgetting them. Allah Almighty says about the polytheists:{they forgot the message, for they were a ruined people."}[Surat al-Furqān: 18]Or in abandoning the Qur'an in any form of abandonment. There is a strict warning against that in the Qur'an. Allah Almighty says:{The Messenger said, "O my Lord, my people have taken this Qur'an as a thing to be abandoned."}How can a rational person abandon the words of His Lord?!The Qur'an is the soul and light of life, It is a Book that guides to that which is most upright. Its follower can never go astray or become miserable. It is a book that Allah made to be a cure and mercy, and a source of power and honor to this nation. If abandoning the Qur'an was what our beloved Prophet complained to Allah of, then it would be utter failure on our part to fall into that. Let us beware of abandoning it in any form of abandonment. Let us not abandon believing in it, while it is one of the six pillars of faith, as Allah Almighty says:{Do you take this discourse lightly, and instead [of thanking Allah] for the provision you are given, you show ingratitude?}[Surat al-Wāqi'ah: 81, 82]Let us not abandon listening to it by engaging in listening to singing and idle amusement. Let us not abandon reciting it by not reading it in full at least once a month. Al-Bukhāri narrated that the Messenger of Allah (may Allah's peace and blessings be upon him) said:"Complete the recitation of the Qur'an in one month…" until he said: "Then, recite it in seven days, and not in less than that. "Let us not abandon contemplating the Qur'an and comprehending it and learning what it contains of guidance in beliefs, morals, practical worship, rulings and laws, and all other contents. Allah Almighty says:{This is a blessed Book that We have sent down to you [O Prophet] so that they may reflect upon its verses, and so that people of understanding may take heed.}[Surat Sād: 29]Let us not abandon adhering to the Qur'an in our actions and complying to its commands and prohibitions. Allah Almighty only revealed it so that we would follow what it contains. Allah Almighty says:{Follow [O mankind] what has been sent down to you from your Lord, and do not follow any guardians besides Him. Little it is that you take heed!} [Surat al-A'rāf: 3]Let us not abandon referring to the Qur'an for judgment in all aspects of our lives by turning to man-made laws, which is one of the main characteristics of the hypocrites. Allah Almighty says:{Have you not seen [O Prophet] those who claim that they believe in what has been sent down to you and what was sent down before you, yet they seek the judgment of Tāghoot [false judges], even though they were commanded to reject them? Satan wants to lead them far astray.When it is said to them, "Come to what Allah has sent down and to the Messenger," you will see the hypocrites turn away from you in aversion.}[Surat an-Nisā': 60, 61]Let us not abandon using the Qur'an as a means of healing the diseases of the hearts and bodies and resorting instead to sorcerers to use their magic and spells as medicine. In brief, any kind of abandonment of the Qur'an is a loss for us, even though some kinds are more severe than others. Because people are distant from the Qur'an nowadays, their hearts have become hard, Satan has gained control over them, and weakness has infested their creed and religiosity. Blessings and mercies are much less, while calamities and afflictions are much more. This treatise is an outcry to one's beloved, screaming out to them the words of Allah Almighty: {Has the time not yet come for those who believe that their hearts should be humbled at the remembrance of Allah and to the truth that has been revealed? And that they should not be like those who were given the Scripture before, whose hearts grew hard after the passage of long time, and many of them were evildoers.}[Surat al-Hadīd: 16]

{Who does greater wrong than one who is reminded of the verses of his Lord, then turns away from them? We will surely take vengeance upon the wicked.}

[Surat as-Sajdah: 22]

Or in forgetting them. Allah Almighty says about the polytheists:

{they forgot the message, for they were a ruined people."}

[Surat al-Furqān: 18]

Or in abandoning the Qur'an in any form of abandonment. There is a strict warning against that in the Qur'an. Allah Almighty says:

{The Messenger said, "O my Lord, my people have taken this Qur'an as a thing to be abandoned."}

How can a rational person abandon the words of His Lord?!

The Qur'an is the soul and light of life, It is a Book that guides to that which is most upright. Its follower can never go astray or become miserable. It is a book that Allah made to be a cure and mercy, and a source of power and honor to this nation.

If abandoning the Qur'an was what our beloved Prophet complained to Allah of, then it would be utter failure on our part to fall into that. Let us beware of abandoning it in any form of abandonment. Let us not abandon believing in it, while it is one of the six pillars of faith, as Allah Almighty says:

{Do you take this discourse lightly,

and instead [of thanking Allah] for the provision you are given, you show ingratitude?}

[Surat al-Wāqi'ah: 81, 82]

Let us not abandon listening to it by engaging in listening to singing and idle amusement. Let us not abandon reciting it by not reading it in full at least once a month. Al-Bukhāri narrated that the Messenger of Allah (may Allah's peace and blessings be upon him) said:

"Complete the recitation of the Qur'an in one month…" until he said: "Then, recite it in seven days, and not in less than that."

Let us not abandon contemplating the Qur'an and comprehending it and learning what it contains of guidance in beliefs, morals, practical worship, rulings and laws, and all other contents. Allah Almighty says:

{This is a blessed Book that We have sent down to you [O Prophet] so that they may reflect upon its verses, and so that people of understanding may take heed.}

[Surat Sād: 29]

Let us not abandon adhering to the Qur'an in our actions and complying to its commands and prohibitions. Allah Almighty only revealed it so that we would follow what it contains. Allah Almighty says:

{Follow [O mankind] what has been sent down to you from your Lord, and do not follow any guardians besides Him. Little it is that you take heed!} [Surat al-A'rāf: 3]

Let us not abandon referring to the Qur'an for judgment in all aspects of our lives by turning to man-made laws, which is one of the main characteristics of the hypocrites. Allah Almighty says:

{Have you not seen [O Prophet] those who claim that they believe in what has been sent down to you and what was sent down before you, yet they seek the judgment of Tāghoot [false judges], even though they were commanded to reject them? Satan wants to lead them far astray.

When it is said to them, "Come to what Allah has sent down and to the Messenger," you will see the hypocrites turn away from you in aversion.}

[Surat an-Nisā': 60, 61]

Let us not abandon using the Qur'an as a means of healing the diseases of the hearts and bodies and resorting instead to sorcerers to use their magic and spells as medicine. In brief, any kind of abandonment of the Qur'an is a loss for us, even though some kinds are more severe than others. Because people are distant from the Qur'an nowadays, their hearts have become hard, Satan has gained control over them, and weakness has infested their creed and religiosity. Blessings and mercies are much less, while calamities and afflictions are much more.

This treatise is an outcry to one's beloved, screaming out to them the words of Allah Almighty:

{Has the time not yet come for those who believe that their hearts should be humbled at the remembrance of Allah and to the truth that has been revealed? And that they should not be like those who were given the Scripture before, whose hearts grew hard after the passage of long time, and many of them were evildoers.}

[Surat al-Hadīd: 16]

Let us glorify the Qur'an as it deserves to be glorified, in terms of knowledge, belief, action, and calling to it, in order to attain what Allah promised of abundant blessings, and so that we can conquer all the wicked enemies from the devils of mankind and jinn. Let us not become of those whose hearts have become hardened, and whose spirits have become defeated, and whose minds have been diverted from the straight path by the devils of mankind and jinn because they distanced themselves from the speech of their Lord; the Qur`an, which can never be challenged by anything that human beings say or do.

May Allah Almighty make me and everyone who reads this treatise and contributes to spreading it among the companions of the Qur'an, who are honored by Allah, who will be awarded {gardens and rivers, in a seat of honor near a Sovereign, Capable One}, without reckoning or punishment. Verily He is All-Capable of this. All praise be to Him, for what He grants of success, generosity, and favor.

This book was completed on Saturday, 30th of Ramadan, 1441 Hijri, in the sacred precincts of Mecca, may Allah increase it in nobility.

- Magnificence of the Noble Qur'an 1
  - Introduction 2
  - The Word of Allah, the Glorified and Exalted 2
  - The Qur'an is Exalted and Protected 3
  - The Magnificence of its Descent as Revelation 4
  - A Heavy Word 5
  - There is no Doubt Therein 5
  - A Verification and a Criterion 6
  - Eternal Preservation 7
  - The Most Miraculous Sign of the Message of Islam 7
  - A Clarification for all Things 8
  - The Magnificence of the Names and Attributes of the Qur'an 9
  - A Wise Book 10
  - A Blessed Remembrance 10
  - A Reminder to the Worlds 11
  - A Spirit by the Command of Allah 12
  - But We Made it a Light 13
  - It Guides to What is Most Upright 15
  - He will not go astray nor be miserable 17
  - Healing and Mercy 19
  - A Trade that will never fail 22
  - A Rope of Rescue for the one who holds on to it 24
  - A Book wherein you are mentioned 26
  - The Intercessor Whose Intercession is Accepted 27
  - In conclusion, I say that my people have abandoned this Qur'an 29

CPSIA information can be obtained
at www.ICGtesting.com
Printed in the USA
BVHW031415230722
642857BV00011B/966